First Certificate Testbuilder

Tony D Triggs

WITH ANSWER KEY

Heinemann English Language Teaching
A division of Reed Educational and Professional Publishing Limited,
Halley Court, Jordan Hill, Oxford OX2 8EJ

OXFORD MADRID FLORENCE ATHENS PRAGUE
SÃO PAULO MEXICO CITY CHICAGO PORTSMOUTH(NH)
TOKYO SINGAPORE KUALA LUMPUR MELBOURNE
AUCKLAND JOHANNESBURG IBADAN GABORONE

ISBN   0 435 24492 2 (with key)
          0 435 24493 0 (without key)

Text © Tony D Triggs 1996
Design and illustration © Reed Educational and Professional
Publishing Limited 1996
First published 1996

This book is dedicated to Kathy Triggs and all EFL teachers.

Designed by Giles Davies
Illustrated by: Kathy Baxendale, Jerry Collins, Gillian Martin

The publishers would like to thank Sara Katsonis, Dave Briggs, The
Lake School of English, Oxford, The Oxford Academy, Oxford.

The author would like to thank Kathy Triggs, Donna Triggs and all
those who have trialled these tests.

The authors and publishers would like to thank the following for their
kind permission to reproduce copyright material: BBC Worldwide
Ltd. for an extract from Geoff Hamilton's Gardening column in
Radio Times, 4th March 1995 p7; Curtis Brown Ltd. on behalf of the
Estate of Sir Winston Churchill for extracts from My Early Life ©
Winston S. Churchill p90; John Johnson Ltd. on behalf of the author
for an extract from No Angels by Francesca Enns p10; D. Kvasnika,
pp170–2; Laurence & Wishart Ltd. London, for extracts from The
Ragged Trousered Philanthropists (1955) by Robert Tressell p66;
PGL Adventure for their advertisement p17; Penguin books Ltd. for
extracts from Island of Dreams by T.Williams, published by Signet
Books 1994 p36; The Reader's Digest Association Ltd. London, for
an adpated extract from The World's Last Mysteries 1977 p35; ©
UCLES/K&J for sample answer sheets pp125–8.

The authors and publishers would like to thank the following for
permission to reproduce the following photographs: Aspect Picture
Library p123(t); Sally and Richard Greenhill p117; International
Stock Exchange p118(b); Powerstock pp120(b), 121(t&b), 124(t);
Tony Stone Images pp118(t), 119(t), 122(b), 123(b), 124(b); M.
Barlow/Trip p120(t), M. Jacobs/Trip p122(t).

Printed and bound in Great Britain by Thomson Litho,
East Kilbride, Scotland

97 98 99 00 10 9 8 7 6 5 4 3

CONTENTS

Introduction	4

TEST ONE

Paper 1
Part 1 — 6
Further Practice — 8
Part 2 — 10
Part 3 — 12
Further Practice — 14
Part 4 — 15

Paper 2
Parts 1 & 2 — 17
Further Practice — 18

Paper 3
Part 1 — 19
Part 2 — 20
Further Practice — 21
Part 3 — 22
Part 4 — 23
Further Practice — 24
Part 5 — 25

Paper 4
Part 1 — 26
Part 2 — 27
Parts 3 & 4 — 28
Further Practice — 29

Paper 5
Parts 1 & 2 — 30
Parts 3 & 4 — 31
Further Practice — 32

TEST TWO

Paper 1
Part 1 — 34
Part 2 — 36
Further Practice — 38
Part 3 — 40
Further Practice — 41
Part 4 — 43
Further Practice — 45

Paper 2
Parts 1 & 2 — 46
Further Practice — 47

Paper 3
Part 1 — 48
Further Practice — 49
Part 2 — 50
Part 3 — 51
Further Practice — 52
Part 4 — 54
Part 5 — 55

Paper 4
Part 1 — 56
Part 2 — 57
Parts 3 & 4 — 58
Further Practice — 59

Paper 5
Parts 1 & 2 — 60
Parts 3 & 4 — 61
Further Practice — 62

TEST THREE

Paper 1
Part 1 — 63
Further Practice — 65
Part 2 — 66
Part 3 — 68
Further Practice — 69
Part 4 — 70

Paper 2
Parts 1 & 2 — 72
Further Practice — 73

Paper 3
Part 1 — 74
Part 2 — 75
Further Practice — 76
Part 3 — 77
Part 4 — 78
Part 5 — 79
Further Practice — 80

Paper 4
Part 1 — 81
Part 2 — 82
Parts 3 & 4 — 83
Further Practice — 84

Paper 5
Parts 1 & 2 — 85
Parts 3 & 4 — 86
Further Practice — 87

TEST FOUR

Paper 1
Part 1 — 88
Part 2 — 90
Further Practice — 92
Part 3 — 94
Part 4 — 95
Further Practice — 97

Paper 2
Parts 1 & 2 — 99
Further Practice — 100

Paper 3
Part 1 — 102
Further Practice — 103
Part 2 — 104
Part 3 — 105
Further Practice — 106
Part 4 — 107
Part 5 — 108
Further Practice — 109

Paper 4
Part 1 — 110
Part 2 — 111
Parts 3 & 4 — 112
Further Practice — 113

Paper 5
Parts 1 & 2 — 114
Parts 3 & 4 — 115
Further Practice — 116

Photographs (Paper 5) — 117
Specimen answer sheets — 125
Key and explanation — 129
Listening scripts — 154

INTRODUCTION

The First Certificate Testbuilder is more than a book of practice tests; it offers students 'tests that teach'. This teaching function is achieved in part through sections of Further Practice and Guidance. These sections review the questions in the practice tests, helping students to reconsider their answers and increasing their chance of getting them right. This review promotes genuine understanding: students will understand why things are right (and alternatives wrong), and be able to carry this understanding forwards to the examination room.

The edition with answer key helps to further the learning process. Answers are often accompanied by an explanation of why they are right – and why others are wrong.

As well as promoting understanding the book promotes confidence. When checking their answers, students find that the Further Practice and Guidance sections have enabled them to score more highly than they might have expected. Since their scores reflect growing language skills (and experience of FCE question types) a heightened sense of confidence is fully justified.

The tests are designed to reflect the actual FCE examination as closely as possible. However, the sample questions and answers given in the real exam are imitated in Test 1 only. This is because in working through Test 1 and its Further Practice and Guidance sections, students will become completely conversant with what is required.

Their rigorous authenticity means that the tests are all of a similar standard and make similar demands.

Note: Certain factual materials have been specially devised for these practice tests and should not be relied on for journey planning or other practical purposes.

Using the First Certificate Testbuilder

Either:
● Work through the book page by page, perhaps under exam conditions, until the end of a Further Practice and Guidance section. Then go back over the relevant part(s) of the test and use what has been learned in the Further Practice and Guidance section to review and check, and possibly change, the answers given in the relevant part(s) of the test.

Or:
● Vary the order.
Students may wish to do some of the Further Practice and Guidance pages immediately before or after the question(s) to which they apply, rather than waiting until they reach these pages. In addition, teachers may wish to cover the Further Practice and Guidance pages as discussion or pair work, or ask students to prepare them before class.

The First Certificate in English

Paper 1: Reading (1 hour 15 minutes)

● The paper will consist of four parts, each containing one text of 350–700 words or, in the case of Part 4, two or more shorter related texts.
● There will be a total of 35 questions of the following types: gapped text, multiple choice and multiple matching.
● Collectively, these questions will test the candidates' ability to understand the gist, main points, detail, structure and meaning of the passages given.

Paper 2: Writing (1 hour 30 minutes)

There will be one compulsory task and four tasks from which candidates select one. Each task should be completed in 120–180 words.

● The compulsory task will involve the writing of a transactional letter. The paper will specify the purpose and audience of the letter, both by means of the rubric and through one or more short texts and/or one or more visual prompts.
● For their second task, candidates will typically be able to choose between writing a specified
– article

– informal/non-transactional letter
– discursive, descriptive or narrative composition or short story.

They will always have the option to write on a prescribed background reading text.

Throughout Paper 2, the rubrics and other data will generally indicate the audience for whom each piece is intended. This has implications for style, and appropriate style, as well as completing the task set, is an important factor which examiners take into account in their marking.

Paper 3: Use of English (1 hour 30 minutes)

- The paper will consist of five parts, with a total of 65 questions in all.

- The parts of the paper will be as follows:

  – a modified cloze text with 15 gaps. The text will be followed by 15 four-option multiple choice questions. The emphasis will be on vocabulary.

  – a modified cloze text with 15 gaps. This will differ from the previous cloze in providing candidates with 'open' choices; there will not be any lists of words from which to select. The emphasis will be on grammar and vocabulary;

  – 10 discrete transformation items. Each of the given sentences is followed by a gapped alternative version, and in filling in this gap the candidate must include a given word. The emphasis will be on grammar and vocabulary.

  – an error correction exercise based on a 15-line text. Some lines contain an extra, unwanted word which must be identified and correct lines must be marked with a tick. The emphasis will be on grammar.

  – a word formation exercise based on a text with 10 gaps. Candidates must fill each gap by forming a word from a given 'stem'. The emphasis will be on vocabulary.

Paper 4: Listening (about 40 minutes)

- The paper will be in four parts, each with a recorded text or texts and associated comprehension tasks. There will be 30 questions altogether.
- Texts will include monologues (such as public announcements and excerpts from speeches, stories or anecdotes) and exchanges (such as excerpts from discussions, interviews or

plays). Each text is heard twice.
- Tasks will be drawn from the following types:
  – multiple choice
  – note taking
  – blank filling
  – multiple matching
  – selection from two or three possible answers (such as true or false or speaker's identity).
- Candidates will indicate their answers on an answer sheet, either by shading lozenges or by writing the requisite word or words.

Answer sheets like the ones used for Papers 1, 3 and 4 are illustrated on pages 125–127.

Paper 5: Speaking (about 15 minutes)

Details of this paper are given in the Further Practice and Guidance section on page 32.

Note: Although the examination is described above and exemplified throughout this book, there is no substitute for reading the question paper carefully in the examination room. For example, a cloze question (as in Paper 3 Part 2) may include the sentence 'There was .... there.' If 'nobody' fits the passage it will score the mark, but what about 'no one'? It fits just as well but will it score? If the question paper asks for a single word in each space it probably won't!

Keep calm, read the instructions and do your best!

Marking the practice tests

In the actual examination all five papers have equal weighting (40 marks each), giving a total of 200. The following advice is designed to help students or teachers to assess the practice tests in a similar way.

Paper 1 (35 questions): Give a mark for each right answer and scale scores up (ie multiply by 40/35 or 8/7).
Paper 2 (two tasks): Mark each task out of 20 marks. No scaling up or down is required as the mark will be out of 40 already.
Paper 3 (65 questions): Give a mark for each right answer and scale scores down (ie multiply by 40/65 or 8/13).
Paper 4 (30 questions): Give a mark for each right answer and scale scores up (ie multiply by 40/30 or 4/3).
Paper 5 Score out of 40. No scaling up or down is required. Grammar, vocabulary, pronunciation, interactive communication and task achievement should all be assessed.

TEST ONE

PAPER 1 READING

You are going to read a magazine article about growing potatoes. Choose the most suitable heading from the list A–I for each part (1–7) of the article. There is one extra heading which you do not need to use. There is an example at the beginning (0).

A Buying your seed potatoes.

B The best of the new varieties.

C The pick of the bunch.

D Green cousins.

E Squeeze them in!

F A heavy crop.

G Fashions in food.

H A matter of opinion.

I Getting them started.

Before you check your answers, go on to pages 8 and 9.

Grow your own

0	H

In 1829, the great writer, politician, agriculturalist and gardener William Cobbett wrote of potatoes, 'I never eat them myself, finding so many other things far preferable.'
5 Well, we're all entitled to our personal views, and my own opinion of potatoes is very much higher than Cobbett's.

1	

Nowadays, potatoes are the 'in' thing so far as health is concerned. In the 60s and 70s we were
10 told to avoid them at all costs for fear of getting fat, but now, thank goodness, they have been re-invented by the dieticians as a source of fibre and vitamins. Sensible people, like you and me, have always eaten them because they taste so
15 good.

2	

Potatoes come in various shapes and sizes, growing at different speeds and maturing at different times in the summer. Maincrop potatoes take up a lot of room, but if your
20 garden is small don't give them up – just get an allotment. You won't regret it, especially when your envious neighbours see you returning proudly home, your wheelbarrow heaped with gleaming specimens.

3	

25 Early potatoes are far more compact. Tastewise, they're a different vegetable from the ones you buy in the shops, and a 'must' for all gardens. If you haven't the room for a vegetable plot, plant individual tubers in the flower border. Home-
30 grown, fresh-dug earlies will more than reward your ingenuity.

4	

If the idea of mixing potatoes and flowers sounds bizarre, you should bear in mind that potatoes make very attractive foliage plants.
35 They're closely related to tomatoes, which when first introduced into Britain were thought to be poisonous and grown for decoration only. The fruits were called love apples!

5	

Buy tubers in the early spring, choosing the smallest you can find, and put them in a cool 40 place to develop shoots. Plant them in March with the maincrop varieties 50 cm apart and the earlies 40 cm apart. Give them a nice warm covering of soil –10 cm is about the right depth.

6	

If you want to try some of the newer varieties 45 see my guide to the best, below. Remember, though, that they vary in vigour, depending on locality, and my comments apply to the south of England. Many of these varieties are available in garden centres, but for the most modern ones 50 you may have to buy by mail order. Whatever you do, buy carefully; the best seed potatoes are small and obviously ready to sprout.

7	

New Potato Varieties	Colour	Size	Yield
Maincrop			
Kestrel	red	large	good
Marfona	white	large	heavy
Nadine	white	med	fair
Red Craigs Royal	red	med	heavy
Sante	white	med	good
Valor	white	med	good
Wilja	white	med	heavy
Salad			
Belle de Fontenay	white	med	med
Charlotte	white	med	low
Linzer Delikatess	white	med	heavy
Pink Fir Apple	white	med	med
Ratte	white	large	heavy
Early			
Accent	white	large	heavy
Foremost	white	med	med
Home Guard	white	large	med

A DETAILED STUDY

The questions below will help you to make sure that you have chosen the correct options for questions 1–7 on pages 6 and 7.

Question 1 Look at the second paragraph of the text and answer these questions.
1 What is meant by saying that potatoes are now the 'in' thing?

....

....

2 According to the passage, what is the difference between 'sensible people' and other people?

....

....

Question 2 Look at the third paragraph and answer this question.
The passage mentions a wheelbarrow full of potatoes but it calls them 'gleaming specimens'. What is the author saying about these particular potatoes?

....

....

Question 3 Look at the fourth paragraph and answer these questions.
1 What does 'ingenuity' mean?

....

....

2 What example of ingenuity does the passage mention?

....

....

3 Why might a gardener use ingenuity in this way?

....

....

Question 4 Look at the fifth paragraph and answer these questions.
1 According to the passage, which two plants are relatives?

....

....

2 Which relatives (such as uncles or aunts) are named in the options A–I?

....

....

3 Which adjective is used to describe them and why is it used?

....

....

FURTHER PRACTICE AND GUIDANCE

Question 5 Look at the sixth paragraph and answer this question.
What do gardeners encourage tubers to do before planting them?

....

....

Question 6 Look at the seventh paragraph and answer these questions.
1 In the third sentence of the paragraph the author refers to 'these varieties'. What word used earlier could be used again here instead of 'these'?

....

....

2 This third sentence tells the reader how (or where) to do something. What is it?

....

....

Question 7 Look at the table at the end of the text and answer these questions.
1 Which sentence earlier in the passage refers to this table?

....

....

2 Suggest a title for this table based on that sentence.

....

....

Now check your answers to these questions and reconsider your answers to Part 1 on pages 6 and 7. Then check your answers to Part 1.

PART 2

You are going to read a teacher's memories of a class she taught. For questions 8–15, choose the answer (A, B, C or D) which you think fits best according to the text.

Halliday's writing leaned very much back to the left. He was the only pupil in the class who wrote in this way. He was a nuisance in poetry lessons as he would giggle and make faces and could never be persuaded to read aloud. His silly behaviour made me believe that he didn't like poetry. However, when I gave
5   the class a test in which they had to write down some poetry they had learned by heart, Halliday seemed to know the most.

Halliday had a special dislike for art and I allowed him to read during this period. He never volunteered for drama and refused to make a speech. Football was the one thing at which he excelled, but the sports teacher decided that he did not assert
10   himself enough and he made another boy captain. This boy – his name was John Jones – could hardly read or write. All attempts to make him work failed, but he captained the team with amazing skill.

I remember an occasion when he led our school eleven out of the changing rooms for a cup match against our fiercest rivals, the team from nearby Winterton School.
15   The Winterton girls' hockey team had already beaten our own girls' team and this – plus their excellent start to the season – had raised their morale to a fearsome level. Even so, John played like a true professional. Our only scorer, he made good use of Halliday's passes and scored a goal for every two that the Winterton players could manage between them. Though Kingston lost, the match was a triumph for Captain
20   Jones!

In spite of all this, the pupil who impressed me most in the end was David Halliday. He gained my admiration on a day when I had his class for art. They came into the hut shouting and pushing and I sent them out again and told them they would not have a lesson until they walked in properly. They thought it was fun to waste as
25   much time as possible, and they jeered and cheered outside the hut. I let them go on for a minute. Suddenly the noise stopped and in marched Halliday.

'They're all right now,' he said. 'I've got them lined up.' I looked outside and sure enough the pupils of class 2D were arranged like well drilled soldiers; they were in order of size and in perfect line – so still I could see them shivering in the chilly air.
30   'Walk in quietly,' Halliday commanded. They obeyed their superior officer and the lesson began. Halliday himself, as usual, refused to work. 'Can I just sit and have a nap?' he asked. After the help he had given me I could hardly refuse.

8 Halliday stood out from the other pupils because of his

A beautiful handwriting.
B bad behaviour.
C love of poetry.
D skill as a footballer.

9 Halliday failed to be chosen as captain of the football team because

    A he was thought to be lazy.
    B he was thought to be a poor leader.
    C Jones was bad at other things and needed encouragement.
    D Jones was better at scoring goals when under pressure.

10 Who felt really confident at the start of the match?

    A the Winterton girls' hockey team
    B the Winterton football team
    C the Kingston team, led by John Jones
    D John Jones and David Halliday

11 The match was a triumph for John Jones because

    A his team won.
    B he scored all Kingston's goals.
    C he made good use of Halliday's passes.
    D he was chosen as Kingston's captain instead of Halliday.

12 After being turned out of the hut, class 2D started behaving themselves because

    A the teacher refused to let them in until they did.
    B they had to obey their superior officer.
    C David Halliday sorted them out.
    D they wanted to get in out of the cold.

13 David Halliday's teacher

    A admired his memory for poetry.
    B admired his strong personality.
    C realized that he deserved to be captain of the football team.
    D realized that he deserved to read or rest during art lessons.

14 Halliday wanted a nap because

    A he hated art.
    B he thought he deserved it.
    C he was lazy.
    D he had worked so hard organizing the pupils.

15 Which of the following do you think would be the best title for the passage?

    A The Big Match.
    B Jones to the Rescue!
    C A Difficult Class.
    D Halliday Earns a Rest!

PART 3

You are going to read an article about Robin Hood. Eight sentences have been removed from the article. Choose from the sentences A–I the one which fits each gap (16–22). There is one extra sentence which you do not need to use. There is an example at the beginning (0).

Who was Robin Hood?

Stories and rhymes about a band of robbers led by a man called Robin Hood have been popular for over 600 years. Five hundred years ago, a man called Wynken de Worde collected the rhymes together and printed a book about Robin Hood's life. Since then, thousands of other books have been based on the rhymes – as well as television programmes, films and computer games. **0** **B**

The Robin Hood stories were certainly very popular with King Henry VIII, who ruled England at the start of the 16th century. Henry was a child when the stories first appeared in print, but they fascinated him for the rest of his life. **16**

After all this time it is hard to tell how the stories began. Some people think that Robin Hood is a fictional character; others think he really lived, and they argue about which part of England he was from.

17   The idea that they were stealing from rich folk to give to the poor has saved them from being branded as villains. They certainly chose their victims carefully, sparing the poor and picking on those who were wealthy and proud.

18   A porter is someone who has to do fetching and carrying work, and the idea fits in badly with all the other stories about his life and character. Enthusiasts prefer to believe that he spent the whole of his life in the woods. They say that most of the stories about him are perfectly true – but not this particular episode.
19   On the other hand, they cannot explain why anyone would ever invent such a story, which ruins the whole Robin Hood romance.

20   They have studied Edward II's accounts, which show the wages he paid to his workers – including a porter called Robin Hood. In November 1324, Hood received his final payment: 'five shillings because he could no longer work'. **21**   If so, Robin Hood was a genuine outlaw who lived in the reign of Edward II. His career of crime was apparently brought to a sudden end when he was captured and made to work as a servant. **22**

A   Historians have tried to check the facts by looking for clues in all sorts of places.

B   All these things have spread his fame throughout the world.

C   One story says that Hood was captured and made to work as a porter at the court of King Edward II.

D   According to the stories, Robin Hood and his men were thieves who pounced on wealthy travellers in lonely woods.

E   They prefer the idea of a Robin Hood who was free and defiant from birth until death.

F   Even as a child he probably played with a bow and arrow, pretending that he was Hood the robber!

G   We cannot be sure that this is the famous Robin Hood but it seems very likely.

H   As a man he sometimes wore Robin Hood costumes for dances and May Day celebrations.

I   Finally pensioned off in old age, his life did not quite match up to the stories!

Before you check your answers, go on to page 14.

A DETAILED STUDY

The questions below will help you to make sure that you have chosen the correct options for questions 16–22 on pages 12 and 13.

Question 16 Look at the second paragraph of the text and answer this question.
The passage mentions Henry as a child and then it mentions how the Robin Hood stories fascinated him for the rest of his life. Which extract illustrates his adult interest in Robin Hood?

....

....

Questions 17 and 18 Look at the fourth and fifth paragraphs and answer this question.
Both missing extracts come at the start of a paragraph so they will have more connection with what follows than with what goes before. Which of the extracts work best in this way?

....

....

Question 19 Look at the fifth paragraph and answer these questions.
1 Which two extracts have a suitable noun or pronoun to go with 'they' in this part of the passage?

....

....

2 The phrase 'on the other hand' suggests a contrast between what comes before it and what comes afterwards. Which of the two possible extracts fits in best?

....

....

Question 20 Look at the sixth paragraph and answer this question.
What sort of people would have studied Edward II's accounts?

....

....

Question 21 Look at the sixth paragraph and answer this question.
The words 'if so' suggest that the author has admitted that something is in doubt. Which extract does admit to doubt?

....

....

Question 22 Look at the sixth paragraph and answer this question.
Which extract sounds like a rounding off?

....

....

Now reconsider your answers to Part 3 on pages 12 and 13. Then check your answers to Part 3.

PART 4

You are going to read some information about British holiday resorts.
For questions 23–34, choose from the towns (A–E). Some of the towns may be chosen more than once. When more than one answer is required, these may be given in any order. There is an example at the beginning (0).
For question 35, choose the answer (A, B, C or D) which you think fits best according to the text.

Which resort or resorts would you recommend for someone who

likes sunbathing?	**0**	D			
likes history and things from the past?	**23**		**24**		**25**
likes studying nature?	**26**				
likes scenery?	**27**		**28**		
is elderly and likes to take things easy?	**29**				
likes a bustling town with lots going on?	**30**				
likes a swim in a good pool?	**31**				
likes fairgrounds?	**32**				
wants holiday fun and attractions out of season?	**33**				
wants an inexpensive holiday?	**34**				

35 Where has this text come from?

    A a leaflet published by the resorts
    B a book for tourists
    C a newspaper
    D a book about the history of seaside resorts

British Seaside Resorts

Britain is famous for its seaside resorts and, though many Britons now prefer to take their holidays in countries where the summers are sunnier, hotter and generally more reliable, Britain enjoys a yearly influx of tourists from those very countries. Britain's resorts are clearly fighting for their share of trade, and some have developed excellent weather-proof indoor attractions. Here is a selection of
5   places which are well worth a visit.

Blackpool   A
Blackpool is famous for its Golden Mile – a huge stretch of beautiful sandy beach. One of Britain's leading resorts, it boasts two piers and
10   miles of amazing illuminations – glittering lighted tableaux that turn the seafront into a wonderland in the autumn months.
For most of the year, Blackpool's Pleasure Beach offers plucky youngsters the chance to take
15   some terrifying rides. (Older folk can try them too if they so desire. A woman of 100 recently tried the new Big Dipper. She said she enjoyed it – though she didn't want another turn!)

Great Yarmouth   B
20   A little smaller than Blackpool, the town has an even wider range of things to offer. This springs from the fact that the town has other dimensions besides its tourist industry. It is a thriving industrial centre and a busy port, servicing the
25   quest for gas and oil beneath the North Sea. It also has historical attractions and, though recent years have seen a catastrophic decline in its fishing industry, seafood can still be bought in one of England's largest market places.
30   Compared with the ones at Blackpool, Yarmouth's swimming pool and illuminations are very modest. However, there is plenty to compensate for this.

Morecambe   C
35   Once a thriving resort, Morecambe now has a slightly old-fashioned, rundown air. This has its own charm and, for those desiring a relaxing break, it is hard to think of anywhere better. For its modest size, the town has most attractive
40   shopping and eating facilities and some unspoilt surroundings. The Cumbrian coast can be seen from the promenade, providing a scenic backdrop to the happy sight of children playing (or donkey riding) on the beach.
Families and the elderly can enjoy a choice of   45
traditional English boarding houses at prices that reflect the undeserved loss of popularity which Morecambe has suffered in recent years.

Brighton   D
Often regarded as the queen of English seaside   50
resorts, Brighton has class! Beautiful Victorian buildings recall its magnificent past as a fashionable resort of the English gentry. However, Brighton has also moved with the times. While preserving its heritage it has   55
cultivated a huge range of up-to-the-minute attractions, though without the gaudy vulgarity one finds at Blackpool.
On the warm south coast, Brighton is a definite must for sun-seekers.   60

Sheringham   E
On the north Norfolk coast, Sheringham has the air of a place which is gradually coming into its own. The smallest of the five resorts which are featured here, it is gradually developing as an   65
unpretentious and very appealing centre for a wide range of holidays. For lovers of old-style railways there is the preserved line offering steam-hauled trips to nearby Holt, a lovely little town in the North Norfolk Heights. (The train   70
can hardly manage the steep ascent out of Sheringham and heavier trains pass non-stop through the intermediate stations, since if they stopped they might have trouble starting again.)
The Heights rise to only a hundred metres, but   75
they provide a distinct environment for a range of unusual plants and birds, making Sheringham an excellent centre for wildlife enthusiasts.

PAPER 2 WRITING

PART 1

Answer this question.

1   You have three children aged 9, 11 and 13 and you want to send them away for a summer holiday. The advertisement shown below offers something that may be suitable.

Carefully read the advertisement and the notes you have made. Then write your letter to PGL, covering the points in your notes and adding any relevant information about your three children.

Write a letter of between 120 and 180 words in an appropriate style. Do not include addresses.

PART 2

Write an answer to one of the questions 2–5 in this part. Write your answer in 120–180 words in an appropriate style.

2   Write a magazine article discussing the idea that young people these days have too much money.

3   Write a letter applying for a job in England which you have seen advertised in a newspaper. Refer to the advertisement and explain why you think you could do the job well. Do not include addresses.

4   Describe the area where you grew up in a way that would help a tourist to decide whether or not to visit it.

5   **Background reading texts.**
     Refer to an incident in one of your set books and say what it shows about one or more of the characters.

A SAMPLE ANSWER

Read the following sample answer to question 1 on page 17. When you have read it, answer the questions which follow it, giving examples to back up what you say.

> 71B Warden Road,
> Bristol
> BS6 AG2
>
> The P G L Co.
> 708 Penyard Lane,
> Ross-on-Wye,
> HR9 5NR
>
> 8th May, 1996
>
> Dear Sir,
>   I am writing about your advertisement, and I would like to ask more details.
>   I have three children one daughter and two sons who are 9, 11 and 13. The oldest son has been playing football and he likes any sports, and the younger brother keen on fishing, but he doesn't like any sport. My daughter has no experience about activeties because she has an asthma but it is not hard.
>   I hope that they can enjoy this opotunity. If they can join this, would you tell me the place and what kind of activities they can do and if there is any discount for the children.
>   I am looking forward hearing from you.
>   Fathfully,
>   Takako Tanaka

1 Does the letter do everything the question asks? Are any parts muddled or irrelevant?
2 Is the letter arranged and paragraphed in an appropriate way?
3 Are the sentence structures correct and interesting? Are the sentences linked to one another to make the letter flow smoothly and clearly?
4 Is there a good range of vocabulary and is it used correctly?
5 Are the verbs and nouns used grammatically? Are there any other points of grammar that need to be changed or improved?
6 Is the style appropriate?

Now check your assessment of this sample answer.

PAPER 3 USE OF ENGLISH

PART 1

For questions 1–15, read the text below and decide which word A, B, C or D best fits each space. There is an example at the beginning (0).

A flight to remember

I always remember the toy plane that gave us so (0) ..*much*.... pleasure during a sunny summer holiday on the coast of North Wales. We stood in a field (1) .... the top of the cliffs, and time (2) .... again we hurled the little glider towards them, into the warm sea (3) .... It always took a similar flight path, curling upwards, looping the loop above our heads and landing in the grass (4) .... us.

Gradually we became more daring. Each flight (5) .... nearer the edge of the cliffs, and the wind always (6) .... our little plane back. Finally, standing right at the edge, I (7) .... to hurl it seawards with all the power I could muster.

It (8) .... out that I'd made the mistake of defying fate and the elements just once too (9) .... This time the plane failed to return. It darted downwards towards the waves then levelled off a metre or two above the spray. Seagulls flew close to examine it as it (10) .... its unsteady way out to sea.

And that's the last I saw of it. It (11) .... into the distance, with only the flock of inquisitive birds to tell me that it was (12) .... in the air.

I suppose it soon came down and got torn (13) .... by the sea. Even so, our main (14) .... as we turned for home was joy at having (15) .... such a glorious final flight.

0	**A** good	**B** much	**C** great	**D** many
1	**A** by	**B** at	**C** to	**D** up
2	**A** or	**B** yet	**C** and	**D** but
3	**A** wind	**B** draught	**C** water	**D** breeze
4	**A** behind	**B** beyond	**C** nearby	**D** among
5	**A** began	**B** was	**C** flew	**D** travelled
6	**A** brought	**B** took	**C** landed	**D** returned
7	**A** thought	**B** decided	**C** commenced	**D** tried
8	**A** worked	**B** turned	**C** broke	**D** went
9	**A** frequently	**B** much	**C** many	**D** often
10	**A** journeyed	**B** floated	**C** flew	**D** made
11	**A** hovered	**B** went	**C** departed	**D** disappeared
12	**A** now	**B** staying	**C** still	**D** yet
13	**A** open	**B** about	**C** apart	**D** up
14	**A** idea	**B** attitude	**C** feeling	**D** sense
15	**A** ended	**B** achieved	**C** made	**D** produced

PART 2

For questions 16–30, read the text below and think of the word which best fits each space. Use only one word in each space. There is an example at the beginning (0).

Entertainment on wheels

Why (0) ...*do*....... so many amusing incidents occur (16) .... train journeys? I remember the day when a ticket inspector entered the compartment (17) .... six or eight commuters (18) .... sitting. Everyone quickly found their ticket – (19) .... for the man sitting next to me. His (20) .... dived urgently into his pockets, and then he began to search through his briefcase. (21) .... else could see exactly where his ticket (22) .... – he was gripping it between his teeth.

The ticket inspector calmly dealt with (23) .... the other passengers. Then, equally calmly, he drew the ticket from (24) .... the man's teeth, examined it (25) .... a frown and popped it back again.

Once the inspector had (26) .... the compartment, most of the passengers settled down and carried on reading (27) .... morning papers. As for the passenger who'd had his ticket in his mouth, he popped it (28) .... his pocket, looking very relieved.

He was generally quite a friendly person, so to make (29) .... I said to him, 'You must have felt foolish – searching in all your pockets (30) .... it was in your mouth.'

'Foolish?' he whispered. 'Not at all – I was chewing the date off.'

Before you check your answers, go on to page 21.

FILL IN THE MISSING WORD

Look again at questions 16–30 on page 20 and choose which of the four options below best fits each gap. You may wish to change some of your answers to the test after you have done this. However, an answer in the test is not necessarily wrong just because it is not among the choices here.

16	**A** during	**B** in	**C** while	**D** at
17	**A** as	**B** where	**C** while	**D** which
18	**A** was	**B** sat	**C** were	**D** are
19	**A** excepting	**B** except	**C** but	**D** apart
20	**A** hand	**B** search	**C** look	**D** companion
21	**A** Everyone	**B** All	**C** People	**D** Others
22	**A** placed	**B** lay	**C** were	**D** was
23	**A** there	**B** waiting	**C** else	**D** around
24	**A** between	**B** through	**C** out	**D** in
25	**A** giving	**B** with	**C** making	**D** producing
26	**A** departed	**B** left	**C** gone	**D** quitted
27	**A** his	**B** their	**C** some	**D** through
28	**A** back	**B** into	**C** down	**D** within
29	**A** chat	**B** talk	**C** friends	**D** conversation
30	**A** and	**B** as	**C** when	**D** because

Now check your answers to Part 2.

PART 3

For questions 31–40, complete the second sentence so that it has a similar meaning to the first sentence, using the word given. **Do not change the word given**. You must use between two and five words, including the word given. There is an example at the beginning (0).

0   I can't find my shoes.
knew
I wish ...*I knew where my shoes*............... were.

31   Too many sweets are bad for you.
eat
It is .... too many sweets.

32   He had to have his door mended.
someone
He had to .... his door.

33   The box was too heavy for John to carry on his back.
weight
Because of .... carry the box on his back.

34   It was raining so much that I stayed at home.
heavy
The rain .... I stayed at home.

35   He'd forgotten Jill's phone number.
couldn't
He .... Jill's phone number was.

36   The repairs to my roof will be expensive.
cost
Repairing .... a lot of money.

37   I slept until the thunder woke me at seven o'clock.
woken
I .... at seven o'clock.

38   Bloggs had committed a serious crime.
guilty
Bloggs .... a serious crime.

39   He was holding some flowers when he knocked at Margaret's door.
hand
He had .... when he knocked at Margaret's door.

40   The knife was too blunt to cut the bread.
sharp
The knife .... to cut the bread.

PART 4

For questions 41–55, read the text below and look carefully at each line. Some of the lines are correct and some have a word that should not be there.
If a line is correct, put a tick (✓) by the number. If a line has a word which should **not** be there, write the word down. There are two examples at the beginning (0 and 00).

Studying away from home

..._the_...	0	If you're thinking of going away to study, your choice of the
....✓........	00	accommodation will be very important. You may be lucky
....	41	enough to have the chance of to staying with relatives.
....	42	However, this can bring problems as well as advantages.
....	43	Family life may well distract you away from your studies, and
....	44	there will also be the question of what you should pay your
....	45	relatives. No matter how caring they may be and no matter
....	46	how much they will want you with them, they won't expect to keep
....	47	you for nothing. Paying too much or too little can be easily
....	48	lead you to bad feeling but setting the right amount can be
....	49	tricky and be embarrassing. You should also consider
....	50	the matter of satisfying the grant authorities. They may
....	51	distrust an arrangement between relatives and finish up
....	52	paying you less than you need. Believe it or not, there's
....	53	a strange idea that if you're living in with relatives it
....	54	costs nothing either for you or for them. Lodging with
....	55	strangers can often be the best arrangement after it all.

Before you check your answers, go on to page 24.

WORK IT OUT

Extra words easily can get into a passage if the writer mixes up two different items of English grammar or vocabulary.

Both the following sentences are correct.

> He booked in advance and the accommodation was very poor.
> Good quality accommodation is important to a successful holiday.

The first says 'the accommodation' because reference is being made to particular accommodation, not accommodation in general. The second sentence doesn't use 'the' because it refers to holiday accommodation in general. Now can you see why 'the' in the first line of the passage on page 23 is wrong? The writer is saying how important it is for any student to choose good accommodation but the 'the' makes it sound like a reference to one particular student's accommodation.

The following pairs of sentences will help you to check your answers to questions 41–55 on page 23. Study them carefully. They are all correct but they will show you how the writer of the passage has made his mistakes. (The numbers match the line numbers in the passage.) You may wish to change some of your answers to the test after you have done this.

41 He had the chance of going to London.
He had the chance to stay in Paris.

43 The noise of the traffic distracted me from the music.
When the police arrived, they called him away from the phone.

46 Your parents will want you with them at Christmas.
No matter how much your friends want your company, finish your homework before you go out.

47 Haste can lead to accidents.
Haste can be a major cause of accidents.

48 Irresponsible friends can get you into trouble.
Smoking can lead to serious illness.

49 Having a tooth out can be quick and painless.
The car can be used but you'll have to be careful.

53 The family had an *au pair* living in.
I just couldn't bear to live with a dog!

55 First I said no, but then I did it after all.
It wasn't till after it all went wrong that they got a new manager.

Now check your answers to Part 4.

PART 5

For questions 56–65, read the text below. Use the word given in capitals at the end of each line to form a word that fits in the space in the same line. There is an example at the beginning (0).

Nothing to match it!

There's nothing to match the (0) ..*warmth*.. and cosiness of a	WARM
genuine log-fire. The luxury and sheer (56) .... of sitting back	RELAX
and watching the progress of fire and flame is almost (57)	BELIEVE
A log-fire appeals to all the senses. Yes, you can (58)	ACTUAL
taste and smell the (59) .... of newly cut timber – and then	FRESH
enjoy the sight and sound of the minor (60) .... as it burns.	EXPLODE
Logs hiss for a while before they (61) .... burst in the heat,	FINAL
so the moment of (62) .... comes as a climax after lots of	DESTROY
suspense!	
All of this is very (63) .... , and the thing that makes it more	DRAMA
(64) .... than ever is that one's feet are up and one's whole	ENJOY
body is being bathed in tropical heat. It's a (65)	MARVEL
experience!	

PAPER 4 LISTENING

PART 1

You will hear people talking in eight different situations.
For questions 1–8, choose the best answer, A, B or C.

1   You overhear this man in a shop.
He wants to change some paint because

    A he doesn't like the colour.
    B he thinks there is something wrong with it. | **1** |
    C he finds it makes him ill.

2   This woman is complaining at a railway station enquiry office.
She is angry because

    A her train is late.
    B her train has been cancelled. | **2** |
    C she thinks the train service is very poor.

3   These two people are having an argument.
Are they arguing about

    A the climate?
    B the weather outside? | **3** |
    C the snowfall in recent years?

4   This is a conversation between a man and a woman.
Is the man

    A a policeman?
    B a garage mechanic? | **4** |
    C a judge or other official in a court of law?

5   The speaker in this extract is a very keen gardener.
He is talking about his success in growing

    A a type of fruit.
    B a type of vegetable. | **5** |
    C some flowers.

6   In this extract you are listening to someone speaking to quite a large group of people.
Is he giving

    A a history lecture?
    B a talk at a gardening club? | **6** |
    C advice to medical students?

7 This extract comes from a talk on the radio.
Is the speaker describing

    A a piece of music?
    B a magnificent building?
    C a formal garden?

	7

8 In this extract you can hear someone speaking on the telephone.
She wants to book some theatre tickets but she finds that

    A the performance is fully booked.
    B the performance has been cancelled.
    C she can no longer have a special discount.

	8

PART 2

You will hear a conversation between a salesman and his customer.
For questions 9–18, complete the notes which summarize what the speakers say. You will need to write a word or a short phrase in each box.

The computer is made in		**9**
The customer asks about getting		**10**
The salesman says there are stocks at		**11**
The salesman says that engineers arrive to deal with faults		**12**
The salesman says that the yearly charge works out at		**13**
The customer asks about running costs, including the cost of		**14**
Each roll of paper for the printer contains		**15**
and costs		**16**
The salesman says the printers are easy to use because		**17**
The customer asks about all the		**18**

PART 3

You will hear five different people talking about the sort of books they like to read.
For questions 19–23, choose from the list A–F what each one likes to read. Use each letter only
once. There is one extra letter which you do not need to use.

A   Popular non-fiction.

B   Technical manuals.

C   Biographies.

D   Books by well-known authors from the past.

E   The latest fiction.

F   Books on historical topics.

Speaker 1   **19**

Speaker 2   **20**

Speaker 3   **21**

Speaker 4   **22**

Speaker 5   **23**

PART 4

You will hear a conversation between a man called Mr Jenkins, his son, Bill, and his neighbour,
Mrs Smith.

Answer questions 24–30 by writing   **J** (for Mr Jenkins)
                                        B (for Bill)
                            or   **S** (for Mrs Smith)   in the boxes provided.

24   Whose face shows how he/she is feeling?   **24**

25   Who mentions road safety?   **25**

26   Who interrupts other people?   **26**

27   Who feels sorry for one of the others?   **27**

28   Bill is accused of something (apart from causing damage).
     Who makes this other accusation?   **28**

29   Who gets interrupted when he/she tries to explain something?   **29**

30   Whose idea is it to use the recreation ground?   **30**

Before you check your answers, go on to page 29.

A DETAILED STUDY

Listen again to Part 4 of the test on page 28 and answer the following questions by writing either T (for true) or F (for false) in the box provided. This will give you extra practice and help you to check the answers you gave to questions 24–30 in the test. (You may be asked to answer true/false questions in this part of the examination so this practice will make sure that you are well prepared.)

1   Mr Jenkins knocks at Mrs Smith's door.

2   Mr Jenkins is the first to speak.

3   Mr Jenkins says he's told his son not to play in the street.

4   Mrs Smith calls Mr Jenkins by his first name.

5   Bill knows that his father is angry from the look on his face.

6   Bill says hello to Mrs Smith.

7   Bill has a very innocent look on his face.

8   At first Bill denies causing any damage.

9   Bill then says that he and his friends have caused more damage than usual.

10 Mr Jenkins mentions Mrs Smith's ruined roses.

11 Mrs Smith is concerned about Bill and his friends.

12 Mr Jenkins has already complained to Bill about causing damage.

13 Mr Jenkins says Bill will have to pay for the damage out of his pocket money.

14 Mrs Smith refers to Bill's ball being damaged by her roses.

15 Bill says that he and his friends were kicking the ball along the road, not across it.

16 Bill refers to his ball being damaged by the roses.

17 Bill uses the expression 'unluckier bounce'.

18 Mr Jenkins threatens to stop Bill's pocket money.

19 Mrs Smith says the recreation ground isn't far away.

20 Mr Jenkins says the recreation ground is half a mile away.

Now check your answers to these questions and reconsider your answers to Part 4 on page 28. Then check your answers to Part 4.

PAPER 5 SPEAKING

PART 1

Answer these questions about yourself.

Where are you from?
How long have you lived here/there?
What's it like living here/there?
How do you usually spend your free time?
What are your plans for the future?

For Further Practice and Guidance on Part 1 of Paper 5, see page 62.

PART 2

Look at the photographs on page 117 and answer one of the following questions.
Then answer a different question about the photographs on page 118.

What's happening in each photograph? Would you like to be involved?
Which of the activities would you rather do? Why?
Which activity is best for students/elderly people? Why do you think so?

For Further Practice and Guidance on Part 2 of Paper 5, see pages 32–33.

PART 3

Look at the map and answer the questions which follow it.

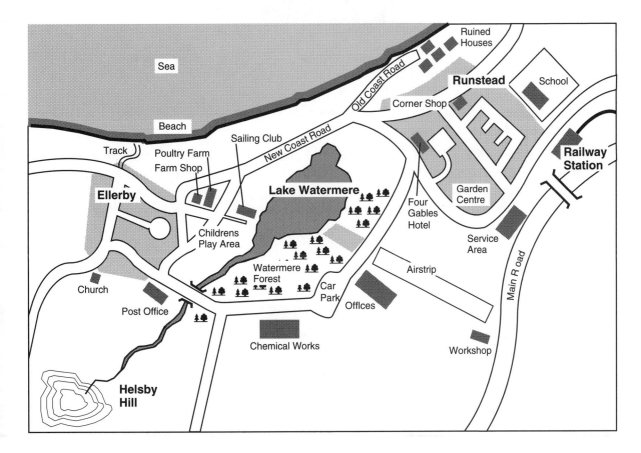

Which village would be more pleasant to live in? Why do you think so?
What new shop, small business or other amenity do you think would do the most to improve
either village?

For Further Practice and Guidance on Part 3 of Paper 5, see page 87.

PART 4

Answer these questions.

How does village life compare with life in town?
How can we preserve the countryside/make towns more pleasant?
Why do people move from town to country or country to town?
Where do you live or think you will live in the future? Is that where you really want to live? What are
the factors that make people live in places which they don't really like?

For Further Practice and Guidance on Part 4 of Paper 5, see page 116.

PREPARING FOR THE TEST

Paper 5 (Speaking) is taken by <u>pairs</u> of candidates, so you won't be alone!

The examination is in four parts:
Part 1 – giving some simple information about yourself (see page 62 for Further Practice and Guidance on this).
Part 2 – saying how you feel about the activities/situations shown in two pictures (see below).
Part 3 – solving a problem or making a decision using pictures (see page 87 for Further Practice and Guidance on this).
Part 4 – discussing with your partner an issue based on the ideas raised in Part 3 (see page 116 for Further Practice and Guidance on this).

Parts 1, 2 and 4 of the test last four minutes each; Part 3 lasts three minutes. There are two examiners in the examination, one who speaks to you and another who listens and notes down marks. Throughout the test, they will be assessing your grammar, your vocabulary, your pronunciation, how naturally you converse in English and how well you do the different tasks.

RESPONDING TO PICTURES

In Part 2 of Paper 5, the examiner gives one candidate two related pictures – which both candidates look at – and then tells the candidate what aspect of the pictures to talk about for approximately one minute. If the pictures were the two photographs on page 117, the examiner would probably ask the candidate to compare the two leisure activities shown and say which of them he/she would rather do and why. The examiner might then ask the second candidate to say whether or not he/she has ever done either activity. The examiner would then give this second candidate two other pictures for them both to look at. As before, the candidate with the pictures would have to talk for about a minute, with the other candidate commenting briefly at the end. It is unlikely that both candidates would be given pictures on the same theme.

Remember: You mustn't just describe the pictures the examiner gives you; you must think of yourself taking part or being involved – or say why you feel that an activity or situation wouldn't be suitable for you. If you were given the photographs on page 118 in the examination, you might start by saying:

'Well, I'd hate the rock climbing because I'm terrified of heights.'

You could then refer to the dreadful drop to the rocks and the sea. All the while you would be making a personal response to what the photograph shows – and gaining marks for doing so.

You could go on to say:

'I'd prefer the other activity because …' **or**
'I wouldn't like the other activity either because …' **or**
'On the other hand, the other activity strikes me as being too dull and safe.'

Phrases like 'on the other hand' can be very useful when you want to compare and contrast different things in Paper 5. Make sure you're good at using them! You should also make sure that you know how to refer to different parts of a scene or picture. To practise this, use each of the following phrases in two different sentences. Try to put the phrases in a different position in each sentence (eg at the start of one and at the end of the other as in the examples below). You can get ideas for most of the sentences by looking at the photographs on page 118.

in the foreground	in the background
in the distance	to the left
to the right	on the horizon
above the man's head	behind him/her
in the centre of the picture	

Examples:
'In the foreground I can see a watering can.'
'There are some yellow railings in the foreground.'

Finally, look at the following alternative ways to start talking about the second photograph on page 118. Which start do you think is better?

a 'Ah! This picture shows someone gardening and in the foreground I can see a watering can. It reminds me of when I had to carry water on my uncle's farm. It tired me out and I'd hate to have to do it again.'

b 'In the foreground I can see a watering can. In the centre of the picture there's a man with a spade – I think he's digging up some weeds. And to the right there's a wheelbarrow with some plants in it.'

Check your answer.

Note: To maximize individual practice, each practice test invites you to give equal weight to <u>two</u> pairs of photographs. However, if you are working with a partner, you can use the photographs on pages 117–124 in the way described opposite.

TEST TWO

PAPER 1 READING

PART 1

You are going to read a magazine article about the planets of the solar system. Choose the most suitable heading from the list A–H for each part (1–7) of the article. There is one extra heading which you do not need to use.

A Too hot for life.

B A place of contrasts.

C Red for danger.

D Gases in turmoil.

E A treat for the amateur.

F A distant wanderer.

G An unseen influence.

H Fact and fiction.

A family of worlds

1	

The solar system is a family of worlds. Nearest to the sun is Mercury, a place where the day is hot enough to melt some metals and the night sufficiently cold to make a rubber ball as brittle as glass. The planet has no atmosphere to scatter light so the sun glares down from a pitch black sky.

2	

5 Venus, on the contrary, has an atmosphere so thick that no one on its surface could ever see the sun. Though the sun is concealed, its energy reaches the planet's surface, turning it into a baking desert where nothing can live.

3	

Beyond the earth and its moon we come to the planet Mars. Its famous redness is due to oxidization – a sort of rusting process that has taken place over millions of
10 years. According to a now discredited theory, intelligent creatures on Mars have dug canals to harness the small amounts of water released when the planet's polar ice-caps melt in the Martian spring.

4	

Jupiter is a giant ice-ball surrounded by an atmosphere of poisonous gases. It is an atmosphere full of storms and turmoil. The biggest storm of all – visible in the form
15 of the Great Red Spot – has lasted for over 200 years and shows no sign of dying away.

5	

Saturn, Uranus and Neptune are giant stepping stones leading us into the unseen coldness of outer space. Saturn is the most distinctive planet of the three, since it has the famous rings which almost everyone has heard about. They form a halo
20 round its equator and no one knows quite how they were formed. A spectacular sight when observed through a powerful telescope, they can also be seen and enjoyed with a simple pair of binoculars.

6	

Beyond Neptune orbits little Pluto. Too small and too far from the sun to receive much light, it reflects so little that it tells us very little indeed about itself. Its orbit
25 sometimes brings it nearer to the sun than Neptune; at other times it swings out into the blackness of space as if it never means to return.

7	

Could there be another planet even further away than Pluto? There are clues that the answer to this may be yes. A mysterious gravitational pull is disturbing the orbits of Neptune and Pluto, suggesting that an unseen world awaits discovery.

PART 2

You are going to read an extract from an autobiography. For questions 8–15, choose the answer (A, B, C or D) which you think fits best according to the text.

The warden led us in single file along a narrow line of paving slabs that ran past the huts. Every so often, four steps led to a front door. We could hear people inside, shouting at children.

'The overcrowding has to be believed,' he said as he shook his head forlornly.

5 We squeezed to one side as a sullen woman passed us, carrying a bucket of coal. She had the look of someone who was old before her time.

The warden went up the last set of steps, opened the door with a jangling bunch of keys, took one off the ring and handed it to me.

'There you are. Home Sweet Home. There's a bath in that hut by the trees; get the
10 key from me when you want one,' he said, and he came down the steps, leaving us room to go up. 'I hope you can make a go of it,' he said. 'At least we've got you a bit of furniture.'

We walked into a square 'cell' with a table and two chairs and a two-seater settee. No two of anything were the same; it all looked like furniture from a charity shop, which
15 I suppose it was. There was a double hotplate on top of a low cupboard, and a dead black stove against the back wall with a scuttle beside it containing a few lumps of fuel. The adjoining 'cell' had a double bed with a pink plastic mattress cover, glistening like wet salmon. There was a cupboard that hung open because the door catch had gone. Inside the cupboard were two meagre blankets.

20 The bedroom was freezing. I struggled to shut the top flap of the window, but it was jammed open by rust. There were bits of yellowing sellotape all round the wall near it, where previous inmates had tried to block the draught with cardboard.

I sat on the bed with my head in my hands, wondering how long we would have to spend here before we found a real home, and noticing, as I glanced sideways into
25 the front room, that a thin film of dust was blowing under the front door.

We took the plastic cover off the mattress because it looked worse than the stains underneath. The blankets smelled, but we had to keep warm somehow.

We had been in this place exactly a week when, on returning in the evening, we went up to our front door and heard children's voices and a transistor radio. We peered
30 round the door at a jumble of people and things and colours. The people turned round and we all looked at each other. The muddle resolved itself into a huge woman and a little man, and two small children. They had a lot of stuff, mostly carrier bags and laundry bags with clothes spilling out, and a couple of buckets full of kitchen equipment which we'd have been glad to have ourselves.

35 They didn't want to share with us any more than we did with them, but that's what the warden had told them to do. We argued about it, though it seemed ridiculous to quarrel over accommodation which none of us really wanted anyway.

8 The place is

A   a prison.
B   a hostel for the homeless.
C   a holiday camp.
D   old people's bungalows.

9 The warden seems to think that the couple's accommodation is

A   cosy.
B   unpleasant.
C   spacious enough.
D   well furnished.

10 The main reason the author feels cold in the bedroom is that

A   there isn't enough fuel for the stove.
B   the window lets in a lot of draught.
C   there aren't enough blankets.
D   the door lets in a lot of draught.

11 The main thing the author notices about the furniture is that

A   it looks or smells dirty.
B   most of it is in poor condition.
C   it is very cheap.
D   nothing matches anything else.

12 The author feels

A   unhappy.
B   optimistic.
C   determined to make the best of the situation.
D   angry.

13 Taking the plastic cover off the mattress

A   releases the smell of the blankets.
B   improves the appearance of the bed.
C   helps the couple to keep warm.
D   makes the bed look worse.

14 The couple's first feeling when they return home to find other people there is

A   confusion and bewilderment.
B   anger.
C   fear.
D   envy of all their kitchen equipment.

15 The four other people are in the accommodation

A   by mistake.
B   because they have been told to share their kitchen equipment.
C   because they have been told to share the accommodation.
D   because a week is up and it is their turn to live there.

Before you check your answers, go on to pages 38 and 39.

A DETAILED STUDY

The questions below will help you to make sure that you have chosen the correct options for questions 8–15 on pages 36 and 37.

Question 8   Look at the whole passage and answer these questions.

1   What is the difference between a warder and a warden? Considering the second word of the passage, which of the options A–D is probably wrong?

....

....

2   What does 'I hope you can make a go of it' in the fifth paragraph mean and which of the options A–D does this contradict?

....

....

3   The words 'cell' and 'inmate' suggest a prison. Why do you think the author has put inverted commas round the word 'cell' and why do you think he uses the word 'inmate'?

....

....

Question 9   Look at the fifth paragraph and answer this question.
'Home Sweet Home' suggests cosiness. Is anything said that contradicts this idea and, if so, how can you explain the contradiction?

....

....

Question 10   Look at the sixth, seventh and eighth paragraphs and answer this question.
Which of the options A–D relate to the bedroom and which relate to other parts of the accommodation?

....

....

Question 11   Look at the sixth paragraph and answer these questions.
1   Which of the options A–D sums up the first thing the author notices about the furniture?

....

....

2   Furniture from a charity shop could be dirty, damaged, cheap or unmatching, and each of these possibilities matches one of the options A–D. However, the author is thinking of one of these qualities in particular. Which of them is it and why do you think so?

....

....

Question 12   Look at the eighth paragraph and answer this question.
Which of the options A–D do the words 'I sat on the bed with my head in my hands' support?

....

....

Question 13 Look at the ninth paragraph and answer these questions.

1 The text implies that something is done to the bed apart from taking the plastic cover off the mattress. What is it?

....

....

2 Why should the smell of the blankets be mentioned now (they were first mentioned at the end of the sixth paragraph)?

....

....

Question 14 Look at the tenth paragraph and answer these questions.

1 How is the other family's appearance first described and which of the options A–D does that support?

....

....

2 Which words in the description and chosen option are similar in meaning?

....

....

Question 15 Look at the eleventh paragraph and answer this question.
Which word from the final sentence of the passage could be added to the previous sentence to make its meaning clearer?

....

....

Now check your answers to these questions and reconsider your answers to Part 2 on pages 36 and 37. Then check your answers to Part 2.

PART 3

You are going to read an article about the Sahara Desert. Six sentences have been removed from the article. Choose from the sentences A–G the one which fits each gap (16–21). There is one extra sentence which you do not need to use.

A water crisis

The Sahara's meagre resources are being plundered right to the present day. This is shown most clearly in the dramatic fall in the region's precious water reserves. The rock is of a type which hinders easy underground storage so the water supply depends on rainfall. [**16**] However, the seriousness of the situation goes far
5 beyond mere seasonal changes.

There is one district where observations go back at least 125 years. Here it is known that wells of the balance beam type were once used in cultivated areas. This way of drawing water is intended for the irrigation of gardens and small plots and works only if there is water not more than about five metres below the surface.
10 [**17**] They have all been replaced by wells from which the water has to be raised by draught animals, because it is now 25 metres down. [**18**]

In a classic example of a vicious circle, shortage of water has led to the digging of more wells to save the flocks and birds. As these have been deepened the water supply has been further depleted. [**19**]

15 The Aïr region was once regarded as the Switzerland of Africa because of its temperate climate. [**20**] Nowadays, though, there are only a third of the palms which existed there at the turn of the century. The amount of wildlife has shown a proportionate fall. [**21**] This is highly dangerous in a world where the overall population is growing rapidly. We cannot afford to lose fertile land.

A   So, too, has the number of human beings who can now survive in the area.
B   This being so, it is easy to understand why it varies.
C   Today, though, not one well of this type exists.
D   This has resulted in soil erosion which then dries out the land still further.
E   Here, then, the water level has evidently dropped by 20 metres in little over a century.
F   It was criss-crossed by valleys filled with palm trees and was thronged with wildlife.
G   Such are conditions in the Sahara Desert in recent times.

Before you check your answers, study the Further Practice and Guidance section on pages 41 and 42.

WAYS OF READING

We all read in different ways for different purposes. If we want a lazy evening watching television we're likely to consult a newspaper or magazine that lists programmes. Of course, we use the headings to help us to skip over days of the week that have already passed, and we also ignore the times of day when we won't be viewing and the channels we don't want to watch. In this way we quickly 'home' on the relevant information and even then we don't read it all – often it's enough to recognize the name of a favourite programme and the time it's on.

This sort of reading is sometimes called scanning. You know what you want or expect to see and you pick it out as quickly as possible.

You may want to do some scanning in the examination. In a way, it sounds quite a risky or careless approach to take but there may be times when you'll find it both efficient and appropriate. For example, it may be a suitable approach to Part 4 of Paper 1. You probably remember the passage about holiday resorts in Part 4 of Paper 1 in Test 1. The first question asked you to choose a resort for someone who liked sunbathing. Look again at the passage (on page 16) and scan it quickly to find the answer. (Do this now, before reading on.)

Having scanned as far as line 59, you probably noticed the answer at once because it occupies a separate paragraph: 'On the warm south coast, Brighton is a definite must for sun-seekers.' Having found this sentence – and thought about it – you probably had no doubt that this was the information you wanted. (You do need to think about what you find because the passage might use a key word like 'sunbathing' only to say that a certain resort doesn't offer that particular activity. When you think you've found the answer look at the context carefully. This will make your scanning safe as well as speedy.)

Throughout Paper 1, the questions and the passages may express the same things in different ways. For example, the question you've just considered mentions 'sunbathing' but the passage doesn't. It does use the first three letters ('sun'), which may be enough to catch your eye, but in many cases the words won't look alike at all; they will match each other in meaning but not in sound or appearance.

Scanning for meaning is harder than scanning for particular words but it's something that you can pick up with practice. Look again at the passage on page 16. One of the questions asks you to pick out three resorts that would appeal to lovers of 'history and things from the past'. Scan the passage again, keeping this idea in mind, and see how well you can pick out the answers. (Two out of three would be good; you can always scan it again.)

The scanning method may not work for all the answers, even in Paper 1 Part 4. Some things may be expressed in ways that are easy to miss. Don't worry: if scanning finds you the obvious answers you'll have more time to read the passage thoroughly to find the rest!

Scanning will probably not be the way to answer multiple choice questions like the ones in Part 2 of Paper 1. The differences between the four options may be subtle and you cannot possibly carry them in your mind as your eye skims over the passage. Also, answering may depend on picking up clues from different parts of the passage. This much remembering, selecting and comparing can't be done in scanning mode!

Even so, a quick first read may reveal the overall shape of the passage, showing you how it 'works' and how it hangs together. This will help you find your way round it as you read it (or read different parts of it) closely to answer each question. Try this not only in Part 2 but also in Parts 1 and 3 which will ask you where missing titles or snippets of text fit into place. See how the passages are structured (put together) and you're half way there! The structures will probable be quite simple, and in Part 3 you'll just have to show how a few last buildings blocks fit into place!

Look again at Part 3 on page 40 and scan it to check its structure. Then remember all the advice above as you tackle Part 4 on page 43.

PART 4

You are going to read some information for gardeners.
For questions 22–35, choose from the plants (A–E). Some of the plants may be chosen more than once. When more than one answer is required, these may be given in any order.

Which of the plants described

flower almost non-stop?

| 22 | | 23 | |

are not very easy to grow from seed?

| 24 | |

make good pot plants?

| 25 | |

have a short flowering season?

| 26 | |

don't grow very tall?

| 27 | | 28 | | 29 | |

will do well in shade?

| 30 | | 31 | |

can be stored over winter?

| 32 | |

need protecting from frost?

| 33 | | 34 | |

have the longest gap between sowing and flowering?

| 35 | |

Garden choices

Seed catalogues feature hundreds of different flowering species. For the person just beginning a garden this can be bewildering, and below are the details of some popular choices, nearly all of which should be sown in the spring. With the exception of busy lizzies, which need a little care, they are all very easy to grow from seed

Dahlias   A

5 These are sturdy plants bearing showy flowers in a wide range of rather gaudy colours. Sow in a frame in April and plant the seedlings out when frosts are over. Dahlias flower throughout
10 the summer and into the autumn. When autumn frosts begin to make them look unhappy, you should dig up the tuberous roots and save them. A frost-free loft, shed or garage is the ideal place. The following spring you can plant the
15 tubers instead of sowing seed again.

Lupins   B

Lupins are hardy perennials. This means that the plants will stay in your garden and carry on flowering year after year. Seed sown in April will
20 usually give you some spikes of colour in the first summer, and year by year the plants get bigger and the flowering stems get taller and grander. Selective breeding has led to the introduction of some fine, bicoloured varieties in
25 some dazzling shades. The short-lived flowers make a real midsummer spectacle.

Busy lizzies (Impatiens)   C

Like dahlias, busy lizzies need to be started off under glass, as they cannot stand frost, and
30 planting out is best done in May. Outdoor flowering ends in September, but beat the frosts and bring your favourite specimens indoors to give your home some winter colour! Indoors they will carry on flowering indefinitely, though
35 you may like to plant them out again when spring returns. Like pansies (below) they do very well in sun or shade, but the soil must be moist. Most varieties grow to a height of only 20 cm or so.

Potentillas   D   40

Potentillas are hardy shrubs. In other words, the woody branches spring from ground level – there is no central trunk. The seed is probably best sown in autumn, in which case you should keep the plants in a sheltered spot until April   45
offers favourable conditions for planting out. Once flowering begins in early summer the best varieties (such as Melton Fire) will stay in bloom almost ceaselessly for years on end while at the same time spreading out to provide   50
ground cover or a low hedge.

Pansies   E

Pansies have a good long flowering season year after year, and some varieties can be sown in spring to give truly splendid results the first   55
autumn. Unlike dahlias and lupins, which can easily grow a metre tall, pansies grow no higher than 10 or 20 cm. Their soil, position and moisture requirements are just like those of buzy lizzies but pansies differ in being hardy. Give   60
them a try!

Before you check your answers, go on to page 45.

WORK IT OUT

In all parts of the examination, and throughout Paper 1 in particular, it is important to read with your mind as well as your eye.

Look again at Part 4 of Paper 1 on pages 43 and 44. Questions 22 and 23 ask you which plants flower almost non-stop. The answers are found in paragraphs C and D. Paragraph C speaks of plants that 'carry on flowering indefinitely', while the plants in paragraph D 'stay in bloom almost ceaselessly'. (The words 'indefinitely' and 'ceaselessly' may be unfamiliar but 'carry on flowering' and 'stay in bloom' give you a very good clue in themselves.)

Once you think you have the answers (and if you have time in the examination) you can sometimes check by finding answers that are definitely wrong. In the case of questions 22 and 23, A and B are wrong since those plants definitely don't stay in bloom: dahlias spend half the year in a dormant state and lupins have short-lived flowers in midsummer. E is tempting, but having 'a good long flowering season' is not the same as 'flowering almost non-stop'; a season is just one part of the year.

For further practice, look at the text on page 44 again and answer this additional question. You may give your answers in any order.

Which two plants described have conspicuous (showy) flowers? | **36** | | **37** | |

Now check your answers to this question and reconsider your answers to Part 4 on pages 43 and 44. Then check your answers to Part 4.

PAPER 2 WRITING

PART 1

Answer this question.

1   You are looking for somewhere to live while studying away from home and you decide to reply to the advertisement shown below.

Carefully read the advertisement and the notes you have made. Then write your letter to the flat owner, introducing yourself and covering the points in your notes. Add any other relevant points.

Write a letter of between 120 and 180 words in an appropriate style. Do not include addresses.

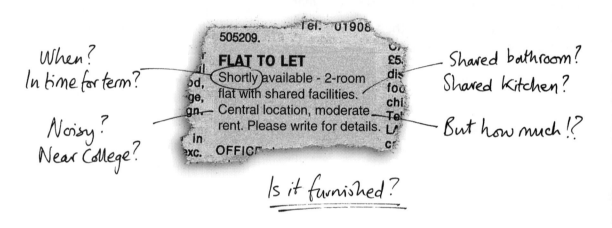

PART 2

Write an answer to one of the questions 2–5 in this part. Write your answer in 120–180 words in an appropriate style.

2   Write a composition or magazine article entitled: *Towns of the Future*.

3   Write a newspaper report on a recent event or notable person in your locality.

4   Write a leaflet entitled: *Getting the most from your local library*.

5   **Background reading texts**
Choose one of your set books and answer the complaint that it's 'full of boring characters doing boring things'.

A SAMPLE ANSWER

Read the following sample answer to question 1 on page 46. When you have read it, answer the questions which follow it, giving examples to back up what you say.

> Dear Mr. Johnson,
>
> I'm writing to ask you for your advertisement in the newspaper. First of all, let me introduce myself. I'm eighteen years old student from Bulgaria. I will stay in England very long time to study. O.K. lets go to details. I want to ask you when I can came to see the flat, and the other thing is are the bathroom and kitchen shared? Another thing I wish to ask you is location. You wrote that the flat is in Central location. I suppose it means that the flat is quite noisy. Also I want to ask you about the rent. How much I have to pay and when. And finally I want to ask you something very important. Is this flat furnished? Please write the answer as soon as possible.
>
> Your Sincerely.
>
> (A. KOTZEV)

1 Does the letter do everything the question asks? Are there any irrelevant or muddled parts?
2 Is the letter arranged and paragraphed in an appropriate way?
3 Are the sentence structures correct and interesting? Are the sentences linked to one another to make the letter flow smoothly and clearly?
4 Is there a good range of vocabulary and is it used correctly?
5 Are the verbs and nouns used grammatically? Are there any other points of grammar that need to be changed or improved?
6 Is the style appropriate?

Now check your assessment of this sample answer.

PAPER 3 USE OF ENGLISH

PART 1

For questions 1–15, read the text below and decide which word A, B, C or D best fits each space.

Putting things right

We all make mistakes. Our company is no exception, and on rare occasions our customers have cause for (1) .... We pride ourselves on our quick, efficient and courteous way (2) .... putting things right.

Please start by having a (3) .... with Mark, our Customer Satisfaction Officer. There's every (4) .... that he can resolve your (5) .... to your complete satisfaction. If goods are (6) .... , he can arrange an immediate refund or replacement and can (7) .... send a van to your premises to (8) .... and replace any bulky item.

Our Managing Director, Mr Fergusson, is also (9) .... by appointment and, if you are still (10) .... with any (11) .... of our service, we hope you will have no hesitation in (12) .... him and letting us know how we might (13) .... our service in future. Our board of directors considers customers' suggestions when they meet each month, and most are (14) ....

All this means that our customers are our first (15) .... – in fact our most important partners in business!

1	A complaining	B complaint	C objection	D refund
2	A in	B of	C by	D with
3	A word	B call	C conversation	D meeting
4	A way	B method	C chance	D intention
5	A need	B breakdown	C fault	D problem
6	A wrong	B bad	C faulty	D broken
7	A just	B firstly	C soon	D even
8	A collect	B take	C obtain	D recover
9	A here	B present	C available	D seen
10	A unhappy	B cross	C sad	D annoyed
11	A respect	B type	C aspect	D kind
12	A writing	B contacting	C speaking	D consulting
13	A raise	B perform	C make	D improve
14	A used	B adopted	C employed	D allowed
15	A concern	B idea	C purpose	D business

Before you check your answers, go on to page 49.

WORK IT OUT

Two, three or four of the possible answers to questions 1–10 on page 48 are used in the sentences below. (The correct word has been included each time.) Study the sentences, then look again at the passage on page 48 and reconsider your answers to the test.

For questions 11–15 write your own sentences for each of the words A–D and reconsider your answers to those questions too.

1 A There's no point in complaining.
      B I take your complaint seriously.

2 A There's just one way in which you can do it.
      B If you don't like my method of teaching, you can go elsewhere.

3 A We had a word on the street corner.
      C We must have been in conversation for half an hour.
      D We arranged a meeting for the following day.

4 C I knew there was no chance or likelihood of winning the car.
      D I've every intention of helping you.

5 A In the famine zone there's an urgent need for medical help.
      D I'm having a problem in understanding English verbs.

6 C My CD player must be faulty – just listen to that humming noise!
      D He picked up the pieces of broken glass.

7 A He was just in time to catch the train.
      C The ambulance was soon on the spot.
      D The doctor was there even sooner.

8 A The postman will collect the mail at five o'clock.
      B You'd better come and fetch your dog – it's wrecking my garden.
      C You can obtain a form at your local post office.
      D They sent a breakdown wagon to recover the broken-down coach.

9 B The chairman insisted on being present at our meeting.
      C Lunch will be available if you book a table in advance.

10 A I'm unhappy with the way my question was answered.
      B I was cross with him when I saw all the damage.
      C I was sad about it but what could I do?
      D He was very annoyed with me when I complained.

Now check your answers to Part 1.

PART 2

For questions 16–30, read the text below and think of the word which best fits each space. Use only one word in each space.

The blue cheese mystery

How do we choose the signs and symbols we use each day? We use green to say go and red to say stop, but just (16) .... if traffic lights were purple and pink. They'd work just the same, so why have we fixed on red (17) .... the colour of warning signals and things like that?

Of course, when (18) .... comes to fashions humans vary their choice of colour quite freely. One year, blue will be a popular colour for home decoration while (19) .... year pink will be all (20) .... rage. Colours for cars change from year to year too.

In (21) .... of all this variation there are one or two psychological facts that (22) .... change. For example, humans perceive things that are yellow or red as being nearer (23) .... things of any other colour. This is important in road safety terms. It means that motorists (24) .... an oncoming red or yellow car (25) .... extra caution. Whereas they might try to overtake (26) .... a blue car's path, they will wait (27) .... the oncoming car is one of those danger colours – red or yellow.

And even (28) .... blue is a popular colour in the home, one (29) .... ever sees a blue kitchen. It's just (30) .... off-putting in the context of food. So why do people eat blue cheese? I just don't know!

PART 3

For questions 31–40, complete the second sentence so that it has a similar meaning to the first sentence, using the word given. **Do not change the word given**. You must use between two and five words, including the word given.

31 The firemen had to break the door down.
necessary
It .... to break the door down.

32 I've never eaten walnuts before.
time
It's .... eaten walnuts.

33 Tom was definitely first in the queue.
doubt
There's .... first in the queue.

34 Mary knows a lot of people in France.
acquaintances
Mary .... in France.

35 Anthony travelled to Spain.
journey
Anthony .... to Spain.

36 The books were so dear that I couldn't afford them.
expensive
The books were .... to buy.

37 I couldn't bear the noise any longer.
put
I couldn't .... the noise any longer.

38 I told John to bring his problems to me.
come
I told John .... his problems.

39 I slowed down at the traffic lights.
speed
I .... at the traffic lights.

40 I couldn't understand what I was reading.
sense
I couldn't .... what I was reading.

Before you check your answers, go on to page 52.

WORK IT OUT

Look again at questions 31–40 on page 51 and then decide which of the four possible answers below is the right answer to each question. You may wish to change some of your answers to the test after you have done this.

31 A It was necessary the firemen to break the door down.
   B It was necessary for the firemen to break the door down.
   C It was necessary to the firemen to break the door down.
   D It was necessary for the firemen had to break the door down.

| | 31 |

32 A It's the first time I've eaten walnuts.
   B It's first time I've eaten walnuts.
   C It's my first time I've eaten walnuts.
   D It's time I've never before eaten walnuts.

| | 32 |

33 A There's no doubt Tom was first in the queue.
   B There's not doubt Tom was first in the queue.
   C There's without doubt Tom was first in the queue.
   D There's can't be doubt Tom was first in the queue.

| | 33 |

34 A Mary acquaintances a lot of people in France.
   B Mary has a lot of acquaintances in France.
   C Mary is with many acquaintances in France.
   D Mary knows a lot of acquaintances in France.

| | 34 |

35 A Anthony went a journey to Spain.
   B Anthony did a journey to Spain.
   C Anthony made a journey to Spain.
   D Anthony has been a journey to Spain.

| | 35 |

36 A The books were too expensive to me to buy.
   B The books were expensive too much for me to buy.
   C The books were too much expensive for me to buy.
   D The books were too expensive for me to buy.

| | 36 |

37 A I couldn't put up the noise any longer.
   B I couldn't put off the noise any longer.
   C I couldn't put up with the noise any longer.
   D I couldn't put the noise up any longer.

| | 37 |

38 A I told John he'll come to me with his problems.
   B I told John to come to me bringing his problems.
   C I told John ought to come to me with his problems.
   D I told John to come to me with his problems.

38

39 A I made my speed reduced at the traffic lights.
   B I reduced my speed at the traffic lights.
   C I reduced my speed down at the traffic lights.
   D I slowed my speed at the traffic lights.

39

40 A I couldn't make sense what I was reading.
   B I couldn't see sense of what I was reading.
   C I couldn't find any sense of what I was reading.
   D I couldn't make sense of what I was reading.

40

Now check your answers to Part 3.

PART 4

For questions 41–55, read the text below and look carefully at each line. Some of the lines are correct and some have a word that should not be there.
If a line is correct, put a tick (✓) by the number. If a line has a word which should **not** be there, write the word down.

Happy quoting!

....	41	Quotations and sayings are part of our language and our way of
....	42	life. As the poet Emerson said, we use of them by necessity; to
....	43	remind ourselves to look before we leap or to avoid crossing
....	44	our bridges before we come up to them. We use them by habit,
....	45	often not realizing we are doing so much, and we all love to
....	46	use an apt quotation to enliven conversation or score a point
....	47	in an argument. This booklet contains over above a thousand
....	48	quotations, proverbs and sayings. Together, they offer a great
....	49	deal of the information, advice, amusement and comfort.
....	50	Emerson wrote 'I hate quotations' so it is doubtful that he
....	51	would have been used this book – but we hope that you will.
....	52	Whether you use it to improve your knowledge more, as an aid to
....	53	solving crossword puzzles, to enrich your own speech or simply
....	54	for idle reading in your spare time, it will put you in to
....	55	touch with some of the cleverest minds of the past and at present.

Happy reading and happy quoting!

PART 5

For questions 56–65, read the text below. Use the word given in capitals at the end of each line to form a word that fits in the space in the same line.

Maths is murder!

By the age of seven I knew that I was a (56) .... at maths and   FAIL

I just didn't have the (57) .... to conquer my problem. It all   PERSEVERE

began when I was two and an aunt who was tired of my

bad (58) .... tried to keep me occupied. She found great   BEHAVE

(59) .... and beauty in numbers and had endless   SIMPLE

(60) .... when it came to explaining them. To my   PATIENT

(61) .... she spent an hour showing me how to write   ANNOY

her address, 11 Smith Road. Later, I (62) .... claimed that   FOOL

two straight bananas somehow made eleven.

After that I was lost. I knew that maths was a (63) .... key to   MARVEL

understanding the universe and that every great (64) ....   INVENT

depends on mathematical formulae. But I'd (65) .... turned   PERSON

my back on number and all its mysteries.

PAPER 4 LISTENING

PART 1

You will hear people talking in eight different situations.
For questions 1–8, choose the best answer A, B or C.

1   John is about to visit Scotland.
He expects that when he gets back home he will

   A   feel refreshed.
   B   find his word processor working properly.
   C   be able to revise his book.

	1

2   You will hear a lecturer speaking.
His main topic is

   A   the problems people have sleeping.
   B   the health effects of tea and coffee.
   C   people's mental abilities.

	2

3   You will hear a man called Mr Waterson being questioned in court.
He claims to have forgotten

   A   the appearance of Mrs Enderby's hair.
   B   the time of day when he last saw her.
   C   the time of day when he was watching television.

	3

4   You will hear part of a conversation between a man and a woman.
The woman ends up

   A   unable to believe the man.
   B   struck by his generosity.
   C   struck by his lack of generosity.

	4

5   You will hear a lecturer addressing a group of students.
He is concerned that the students

   A   shouldn't all try to read the same books at once.
   B   should buy the really important books which he has ordered for them.
   C   should divide up so that they cover the whole of the course between them.

	5

6   You will hear a conversation between two golfers.
The man is losing his golf balls because

   A   there is something wrong with his club or the way he plays.
   B   there is something wrong with his arm.
   C   there is something wrong with his glasses.

	6

7 Listen to part of an interview on the radio.
Mr Fergusson, who speaks first, thinks that

    A cheap houses are the best investment.
    B dearer houses are the best investment.
    C there's no fixed rule about whether to buy a cheap house or a dearer one.

	7

8 You will hear a radio news report about a late night incident in a town.
The incident involved a man protesting about

    A rising water bills.
    B police behaviour.
    C wasted water or electricity.

	8

PART 2

You will hear a man called Mike telling you about his plans for the evening.
For questions 9–18, complete the notes which summarize what he says. You will need to write a word or a short phrase in each box.

Mike knows that Jill is coming to see him because	**9**
She should turn up in about	**10**
Jill used to go in for things like skiing but Mike just	**11**
Two things put Mike off going to a restaurant: one is	**12**
and the other is	**13**
Mike is afraid that overcrowding could spoil a visit to	**14**
Mike wants to take Jill to a special room at	**15**
The things in the room are the wrong	**16**
Mike wants Jill to try the room out but the museum	**17**
In the end, Mike wonders about taking Jill to see Herbert and Muriel, who are	**18**

PART 3

You will hear five people talking about memorable experiences they have had.
For questions 19–23, choose from the list A–F what happened to each one. Use each letter only once. There is one extra letter which you do not need to use.

A	Given the sack.	Speaker 1	19
B	Rescued by the fire brigade.	Speaker 2	20
C	Drenched by a downpour.	Speaker 3	21
D	Covered in paint.		
E	Covered in dye.	Speaker 4	22
F	Wet from a river or lake.	Speaker 5	23

PART 4

You will hear a conversation which takes place on a busy pavement between an inspector from the government, a woman called Mrs Turnbull and a woman who is passing by.

Answer questions 24–30 by writing   **I** (for inspector),
                                  T (for Mrs Turnbull)
           or   **P** (for passer-by)   in the boxes provided.

24   Who makes a mistake about what someone else thinks?   24

25   Who gets a name wrong?   25

26   Who represents a campaigning group?   26

27   Who cares about wildlife?   27

28   Who says the road would only be moved a short distance?   28

29   Who says the road could be raised in places?   29

30   Who thinks he/she is being treated unfairly?   30

ATTITUDES AND FEELINGS

Most parts of the examination can have questions that test how sensitive you are to people's feelings. Don't worry! You don't have to be a psychologist or a mind-reader – all the clues will be there in the language. If someone says 'you've made a fine mess of this' you have to consider what they mean by 'a fine mess'. The word 'fine' is usually a sign of approval, but no one's likely to approve of a mess so on this occasion 'fine' is being used ironically. This means it's being used for effect in a context that shows the person's true feelings.

In Part 1 on page 56, question 4 asked about Jean's true feelings when her friend says he'll buy her a CD or a pair of slippers. She says, 'That's nice. That's very nice', but her hesitation – 'Oh. Oh, well thanks' – and her use of the weak word 'nice' show how dismayed she is that he isn't being more generous, especially after all he's said to build up her hopes.

Of course, people sometimes describe their feelings in a straightforward way. If someone describes an embarrassing event and says how embarrassed it made them feel you can trust what they say.

Listen again to Part 3 of the test on page 58 and answer the following questions about the speakers' feelings or attitudes. Sometimes the feelings are stated clearly and sometimes you have to listen for clues in a sensitive way.

1   Which speakers say they felt embarrassed? ☐ ☐ ☐

2   Which speaker was terrified at one stage? ☐

3   Which speaker enjoys making the story sound exciting? ☐

4   Which speaker accepts that he more or less deserved his misfortunes? ☐

5   Which speaker felt furious at one stage? ☐

6   Which speaker shows the greatest sense of humour? ☐

PAPER 5 SPEAKING

PART 1

Answer these questions about yourself.

How long have you been studying here?
What do you enjoy/dislike about being at school/college?
What do you expect to do when you finish?
What do you hope to do with your life? Do you have any special ambitions or plans?

For Further Practice and Guidance, see page 62.

PART 2

Look at the photographs on page 119 and answer one of the following questions. Then answer a different question about the photographs on page 120.

What's happening in each photograph? Would you like to be involved?
Which form of travel would you prefer? Why?
What are the advantages and disadvantages of each form of travel?

PART 3

Look at the map and answer the questions which follow it.

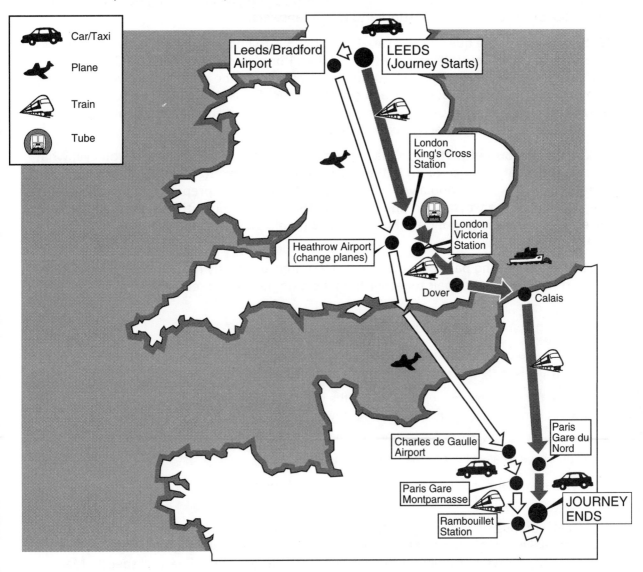

Which of the two routes shown would you use to make the journey from Leeds to Rambouillet?
What are the advantages and disadvantages of each route?

PART 4

Answer these questions.

What do you like or dislike about travelling?
Do you think vehicles are destroying our towns and cities? What can we do about it?
Why do so many people insist on using cars instead of public transport?
What would happen to society if all the world's oil wells suddenly ran dry?

TALKING ABOUT YOURSELF

In Part 1 of Paper 5, the examiner will expect you and your partner to talk about yourselves. He/she will help and encourage you in turn by prompting you and asking questions. You will probably give a mixture of short and longer answers.

Note: The aim of the questions in Part 1 of Paper 5 is to encourage you to give personal information about yourself. The questions in Test 1 on page 30 are based on Cambridge's own examples. The corresponding questions in Tests 2–4 in the book depart from Cambridge's examples, though the aim of the questioning is still to elicit personal information. Varied practice is thus provided and you will be equipped to deal flexibly with the questions asked in the actual examination.

Talking about yourself isn't hard! The examiner will probably ask you where you live, what you do and what you plan to do in the future. You don't have to give a long, uninterrupted speech and you'd be making a very bad mistake if you tried to prepare one in advance. Prepared answers always sound unnatural and they rarely fit in with the question that's asked. Just relax and respond to the examiner's simple questions and prompts in a straightforward way.

Look at the following pairs of sentences. Each sentence is partly right and partly wrong. Put the correct parts of each pair together to make a single, correct sentence.

1   I'm 20 years old and I'm living in London since last year.
    I have 20 years and I've been living in London since last year.

2   I'm studying English in Lexicon College.
    I study the English at Lexicon College.

3   I live at my house on the opposite side of the city.
    I live at home on the opposite half of the city.

4   I don't have a car so I get to the college by foot or by bus.
    I don't have a car so I get to the college on foot or on bus.

5   If I pass my exams, I can be able to take a secretarial course.
    If I pass my exams, I'll be able to study a secretarial course.

Now make up five similar sentences giving true information about yourself; then say them aloud to make a single connected statement. As you speak, make slight changes so that what you say 'flows' naturally – a few slight hesitations are part of natural speech. Make sure you don't rush or your pronunciation will suffer.

Check your answers to questions 1–5.

TEST THREE

PAPER 1 READING

PART 1

You are going to read an article about being punctual. Choose the most suitable heading from the list A–H for each part (1–7) of the article. There is one extra heading which you do not need to use.

A A very vague word.

B Traffic fumes!

C Always some excuse.

D Waiting, waiting!

E An unfair complaint.

F It's up to you!

G Putting friends to the test.

H Getting a lift.

Turn up on time

1

There is nothing worse than someone who is always late. Lateness can be a charming eccentricity – for a little while. The trouble is that Mr or Mrs Unpunctual soon starts causing
5 inconvenience to other people. That's when the cheerful acceptance gives way to scorn and resentment.

2

It's surprising how far the unpunctual person will go to inconvenience others. For example,
10 after accepting the offer of a lift to work the following morning, he or she will fail to turn up at the pick-up spot at the agreed time. There's sure to be a convincing reason: lost door keys, a child with whooping cough, a cat stuck up an
15 apple tree ...

3

The giver of the lift makes sure he's not late. He's made the offer and now he feels responsible for it; come what may he must keep his word. On the other hand, the person who's
20 receiving the favour feels free to turn up 10, 15 or 30 minutes after the time which had been agreed. For him or her they are minutes of hurried activity earning the right to chauffeur-driven luxury; for the driver – the victim – they
25 are minutes of sheer frustration, boredom and wasted time.

4

What's the result of this easy-going attitude? Well, maybe the person who offered the lift gives up the seemingly endless wait and disappears, in which case the latecomer struggles to complete 30
his day's schedule later than ever. Wherever he goes he blames the lift for 'letting him down'.

5

There's another equally likely result. In this version of the story, the giver of the lift waits in loyal frustration at the side of the road for as 35
long as his thoughtless passenger takes to reach the spot. Not only are both of them late for work, but the passenger tells his colleagues about the driver's impatience in traffic queues!

6

So what's the answer? Perhaps there should be a 40
subtle change in how we view time. At the moment we think of it as a very elastic commodity; we make vague arrangements to meet at about a certain time, and no one has a clear idea as to just how far that time will 45
stretch. Will 'about ten o'clock' stretch to quarter past ten – or will it stretch to half past ten? There are no fixed rules.

7

Why not arrange to meet by a certain time and stick to it? Not giving even a minute's grace 50
seems a little harsh, but look at it this way: a train won't wait for a late passenger. People know what the deadline is, they accept that they have to be on time and they usually are. Even the closest friends give up on each other 55
eventually, so they may as well set a giving-up time when they make their arrangement. 'By ten o'clock' should mean 'sorry, but that's when I set off without you'.

Before you check your answers, go on to page 65.

WORK IT OUT

The exercise below will help you to make sure that you have chosen the correct options for questions 1–7 on pages 63 and 64.

Each of the following phrases can be fitted into one of the paragraphs in the text on page 64, though in one or two cases the punctuation needs to be changed. Choose the correct place in the text for each phrase. Give the line number or say what comes before or after.

1   – which is of course the height of injustice

....

2   They find that their patience is being tried and

....

3   They're never short of some excuse!

....

4   as he sits just twiddling his thumbs and waiting

....

5   'He's not very friendly,' the passenger moans. 'He sits there fuming about the delays.'

....

6   So it's up to you to be there on time.

....

7   With a word like 'about'

....

Now check your answers to this exercise and reconsider your answers to Part 1 on pages 63 and 64. Then check your answers to Part 1.

PART 2

You are going to read an extract from a book. For questions 8–14, choose the answer (A, B, C or D) which you think fits best according to the text.

That night as Easton walked home through the rain he felt very depressed. It had been a very bad summer for most people and he had not fared better than the rest. A few weeks with one firm, a few days with another, then out of a job, then on again for a month perhaps, and so on.

5   William Easton was a man of medium height, about 23 years old, with fair hair and moustache and blue eyes. His clothes, though shabby, were clean and neat but the holes in his shoes made it painful to walk.

He was married: his wife was a young woman whose acquaintance he had made when he happened to be employed with others painting the outside of the house
10   where she was a general servant. Easton had been in no hurry to marry for he knew that, taking good times with bad, his wages did not average a pound a week. However, after going out for 18 months they were finally married.

That was a year ago.

As a single man he had never troubled much if he happened to be out of work. He
15   always had enough to live on and pocket money besides, but now that he was married it was different; the fear of being 'out' haunted him all the time.

He had started for Rushton and Co. on the previous Monday after having been idle for three weeks and, as the house where he was working had to be done right through, he had congratulated himself on having secured a job that would last till
20   Christmas; but he now began to fear that what had happened to Jack Linden – a master craftsman – might also happen to himself at any time. He would have to be very careful not to offend Bill Crass in any way. He was afraid that the latter did not like him very much as it was. He knew that Crass could get him the sack at any time and would not scruple to do so if he wanted to make room for some pal of his.

25   Crass, the foreman, was quite without special abilities; he was if anything inferior to the majority of the men he supervised. Even so, he pretended to know everything, and the vague references he was in the habit of making to 'tones' and 'shades' and 'harmony' had so impressed Frederick Hunter that the latter was completely taken in. It was by pushing himself forward in this way that Crass had managed to get
30   himself put in charge of the work.

Although Crass did as little as possible himself, he took care to work the others hard. Any man who failed to satisfy him was reported to Hunter as being 'no good' or 'too slow for a funeral' and was then dispensed with at the end of the week. Knowing this, all the workers feared and hated the wily Crass.

35   Some, by giving him pipefuls of tobacco and pints of beer, managed to stay in Crass's favour and often kept their jobs when better men were dismissed.

As he walked home through the rain thinking of these things, Easton realized that it was not possible to foresee what a day or even an hour might bring.

8   As he walked home, Easton felt depressed because

    A   it had been a bad summer for most people, including him.
    B   he was afraid of losing his job.
    C   he had recently got married, despite his low wages.
    D   his shoes were worn out and his feet were hurting.

9   The fifth paragraph mentions Easton's fear of being 'out'. Is this a fear of

    A   being unemployed?
    B   not having any money?
    C   having nowhere to live?
    D   falling out with his wife?

10   The most senior person mentioned in the passage is

    A   Jack Linden.
    B   Frederick Hunter.
    C   Bill Crass.
    D   William Easton.

11   Crass got his position because Hunter thought he was good at

    A   using language.
    B   managing other people.
    C   understanding colour schemes.
    D   repairing or decorating houses.

12   To keep his job, anyone working under Crass had to

    A   work hard.
    B   give him presents.
    C   take care not to offend him.
    D   make room for his 'pals' (friends).

13   Crass was

    A   a skilful worker but lazy.
    B   not very skilful but hard working.
    C   not very skilful and also lazy.
    D   a skilful man and a hard worker.

14   A good title for the passage would be

    A   Foreman Crass.
    B   An Uncertain Future.
    C   Too Slow for a Funeral.
    D   A Miserable Walk.

PART 3

You are going to read a nephew's memories of his uncle. Seven sentences have been removed from the passage. Choose from the sentences A–H the one which fits each gap (15–21). There is one extra sentence which you do not need to use.

Memories of a man I won't forget!

I wish you'd met my Uncle Bill. He was a tall man – so tall that he could change the bulbs in light sockets while hardly reaching above his head. He said that he wasn't supposed to reach
5 up – it was something to do with a heart condition – and that being tall made life much easier. **15** [   ] Those accessible bulbs were an easy target for that lofty, blundering head of his.

10 I realized from the start that his problem was not so much tallness as clumsiness. He blundered into anything and everything and often had injuries (though not in fact burns) to prove how accident-prone he was.

15 A miserly man, my uncle always stuck replacement soles on his shoes as the old ones wore through, no matter how shabby the uppers became – or how badly he injured himself in the process. **16** [   ] Well, strictly it wasn't the
20 sticking that did it but the razor blade adjustments that followed. In his clumsiness, he nearly always stuck the soles slightly out of position. Once firmly glued they couldn't be moved but at least the protruding parts could be neatly trimmed away. **17** [   ]   25

I can see him now in my mind's eye! There was the sole, slightly out of position, and there was my uncle, his fingers encrusted with firmly set glue. **18** [   ] Then he'd blunder round his house in search of lint and sticking plasters.   30 Vases would topple, ornaments would get knocked off walls. He lived alone but his frequent visitors were used to the commotion my uncle made as he hurried round his untidy house. **19** [   ] Even going to answer the   35 phone could cause calamities and a trail of damage.

20 [   ] No, they were due to injured fingers, banged heads and falls down stairs. As a matter of fact he survived so many serious   40 injuries that in the end I came to doubt that there was anything wrong with his heart at all. **21** [   ]

A   I think he preferred to claim a bad heart than admit to bad eyesight or total and utter clumsiness!
B   He would set to work with his razor blade, and a minute later we'd hear his cry of pain and frustration.
C   My uncle's visits to hospital never resulted from that famous heart condition of his.
D   But how could even a clumsy man suffer injuries sticking soles on his shoes?
E   And that's where the razor blades came in, and all the consequent injuries to fingers and thumbs.
F   However, it also created problems for him.
G   The slightest haste was enough to cause an accident.
H   You should have seen him when he really got going!

Before you check your answers, go on to page 69.

A DETAILED STUDY

The questions below will help you to make sure that you have chosen the correct options for questions 15–21 on page 68.

Question 15   Look at the first paragraph of the text and answer this question.
What the passage says before the gap ('being tall made life much easier') and after the gap ('those accessible bulbs were an easy target for that lofty, blundering head of his') seems contradictory, but which of the extracts A–H makes a smooth link between the two sentences?

....

....

Question 16   Look at the third paragraph and answer this question.
The sentence before the gap is about sticking replacement soles on his shoes. Which extract also talks about this?

....

....

Questions 17 and 18   Look at the third and fourth paragraphs and answer this question.
The sentence before gap 17 talks about trimming spare rubber away and the sentence after gap18 talks about going for first aid equipment. The two razor blade sentences must fit in here – but in which order?

....

....

Question 19   Look at the fourth paragraph and answer this question.
The passage says 'he hurried round his untidy house' before the gap and 'even going to answer the phone could cause calamities and a trail of damage' after the gap. Which extract makes a smooth link between the two sentences?

....

....

Question 20   Look at the fifth paragraph and answer this question.
Which extract mentions what the following sentence refers to as 'they'?

....

....

Question 21   Look at the fifth paragraph and answer this question.
Just before the gap, the passage suggests that there was nothing wrong with the uncle's heart. Which extract mentions his 'bad heart' and suggests why he falsely made out that he had one?

....

....

Now reconsider your answers to Part 3 on page 68. Then check your answers to Part 3.

PART 4

You are going to read a review of some cafés and restaurants in the English market town of Whickham.
For questions 22–35, choose from the cafés and restaurants (A–E). Some of them may be chosen more than once. When more than one answer is required, these may be given in any order.

Which establishment would you choose if you wanted

traditional food?	22	23
low prices?	24	25
traditional English cakes called muffins?	26	
car parking space?	27	
the freedom to smoke?	28	
a long, relaxing evening out?	29	
posh surroundings?	30	
quick service?	31	
the chance to discuss the food with the chef or proprietor?	32	33
home-made food?	34	
the chance to meet an artist?	35	

Spoilt for Choice

Muffin's   A

Muffins are traditional English cakes and it's
fitting that a restaurant as traditional as Muffin's
should choose this particular name for itself.
5 The building, as well as the food, enhances the
atmosphere of tradition and cosiness. The leaded
windows, the blazing log-fire, the pinafored
waitresses, all recall the England of 150 years
ago. My two regrets are that Muffin's doesn't
10 open until the evening and that muffins
themselves don't feature in its varied bill of fare.

An excellent place – it's hard to believe that the
tarmac outside fills with modern cars rather than
Regency horses and carriages. Having seen what
15 they serve, I class the cooks as culinary artists,
albeit unadventurous ones. Give Muffin's a try!

Sandra's   B

Sandra's Café doesn't boast the class and
distinctiveness of its neighbour, Muffin's.
20 Sandra's serves down-to-earth food and drink at
down-to-earth prices. Actually, if I'm strictly
accurate, Sandra's doesn't serve anything: it's
organised on modern, self-service lines and the
lunchtime queue of tray-bearing customers
25 testifies to its popularity. Be warned, though: the
10 minute wait to pay and the subsequent
search for a table can cool your food and dull
your appetite. So can the cigarette smoke that
often fills the air. A place to avoid!

30 ## The Bon Hommie   C

This is an interesting outfit that puts its
customers first. There's a welcome to all, not
least the disabled, for whom the facilities really
are exemplary. The pernickety palate is catered
35 for by a chef who consults you down to the final
grain of spice. The wines are served at the
perfect temperature – that's to say whatever you,
the customer, think is the perfect temperature.
(How they get them exactly right is a mystery to
40 me.)

I said there's a welcome for all, but of course
there's one big qualification to add: The Bon
Hommie is for those with a bulging wallet. The
less well off needn't think of setting a foot inside
these sumptuous premises. The plush velvet   45
carpet and velvetized wallpaper sum it all up,
reminding us by their cleanliness that smoking is
something one doesn't do at The Bon Hommie!
Who would dream of spoiling their palate in the
presence of such superb cuisine?   50

The Tasty Grill   D

This mid-priced restaurant, which grills nearly
all the food it serves, is well worth a try. Though
small, it offers a very wide range of grills: there
are vegetarian nut cutlets, imaginative cheese-   55
and-pineapple inventions – still grilled, of
course! – and much else besides. Ernest
Hambre, the proprietor, concocts some of these
new dishes himself and his friendly smile and
genuine interest in his customers' reactions   60
contrast with the take-it-or-leave-it attitude often
encountered in mid-price establishments.
Needlessly brisk service is the one thing that
tends to spoil a visit to The Tasty Grill. Unlike
The Bon Hommie, it isn't a place for a long,   65
relaxing evening out.

An artist by training and still a painter in his
spare time, Hambre has adorned the restaurant
in the modern art of his native Mexico.

Margery's Tea Room   E   70

Despite the name, this is open from dawn to
dusk and offers, among its range of traditional
cakes and dainties, those piping hot muffins one
finds it so hard to get these days. Believe it or
not, everything is skilfully prepared and baked   75
on the premises by the resident chef and
proprietor, Margery Evans herself.

Lunchtime sees a demand for dull,
commonplace sandwiches. Margery is perhaps a
little too obliging to educate her customers'   80
tastes. There are no real surprises at Margery's
Tea Room, except perhaps that she charges so
little and gives such excellent, wholesome value
– including personal table service complete with
Margery's ever-friendly smile.   85

PAPER 2 WRITING

PART 1

Answer this question.

1 You are interested in staying with a family while studying at a college in England and you decide to reply to the advertisement shown below.

Carefully read the advertisement and the notes you have made. Then write your letter to the family, introducing yourself and covering the points in your notes. Add any other relevant points.

Write a letter of between 120 and 180 words in an appropriate style. Do not include addresses.

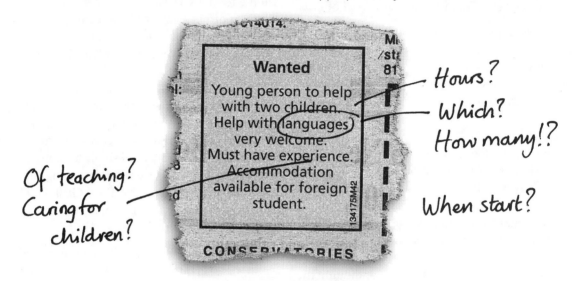

PART 2

Write an answer to one of the questions 2–5 in this part. Write your answer in 120–180 words in an appropriate style.

2 Describe someone you know so that he/she can be easily recognized in the street.

3 As part of a letter to a friend, write a true or fictional account beginning with the words:
It happened like this. I was walking down the street when ...

4 A taxi firm has invited you to comment on someone who wants to work for them. Begin your reply with the words:
I think Pete Hull would make a good taxi driver because ... or
I cannot recommend Pete Hull because ...
(You can base your answer on someone you know as long as you use the name above.)

5 **Background reading texts**
Choose one of your set books. Refer to part of the book or one of the characters in it and explain how true to life this part of the book or this character is.

A SAMPLE ANSWER

Read the following sample answer to question 1 on page 72. When you have read it, answer the questions which follow it, giving examples to back up what you say.

9th May 1996

Dear Sir/Madam

I am writing to you interested in the accommdation you have offered to someone to help with two children. I am a twenty one-year boy and I come from Saudi Arabia, I have been in England for seven months and I have been studying English since I arrive on 9th October 1995

I study business and finance at Oxford college of further education in the evenings and after seven in the evening I am available. I can speak four langußes fluently which are Spanish, French, Arabic and English.

I worked in a nursery school for one year in france after I had worked in Spain as a teacher in a nursery School. I lived with an English family for one year, I used to help them with their children and cooking.

I am enquiring about the time which I should help you with the children and for how long. More over you have mentioned languages but we do not know what languges are requested. I would like to ask about the experience what kind of experience, teaching, or looking after children, lastly I am asking about the accommodation what kind of it and how it is like.
I look forward to receiving your letter.
yours faithfully
Ahmed Salim Balsharaf
Ahmed Salim Balsharaf

1　Does the letter do everything the question asks? Are there any irrelevant or muddled parts?
2　Is the letter arranged and paragraphed in an appropriate way?
3　Are the sentence structures correct and interesting? Are the sentences linked to one another to make the letter flow smoothly and clearly?
4　Is there a good range of vocabulary and is it used correctly?
5　Are the verbs and nouns used grammatically? Are there any other points of grammar that need to be changed or improved?
6　Is the style appropriate?

Now check your assessment of this sample answer.

PAPER 3 USE OF ENGLISH

For questions 1–15, read the text below and decide which word A, B, C or D best fits each space.

Accidentally on purpose

Stamp collecting! What a wonderful hobby! I began when I was only five.
I used to (1) .... for the postman's arrival, always (2) .... to seize
unwanted envelopes and tear off the corner with the stamp stuck on it.

Once – I remember it all too clearly – my mother and father were sunning
themselves in the garden when the post (3) .... on the doormat. I heard the
clatter of the letter flap and hurriedly went to (4) .... There were four or five
envelopes, all with very enticing stamps.

Even at the (5) .... age of five I knew one doesn't open mail addressed to
other people. However, tearing just the corners off the envelopes (6) .... me as
perfectly fair and allowable, and that's what I did. I carefully tore as (7) .... to
the stamps as (8) .... , feeling that even the envelopes, which were addressed
to my parents and not to me, should be treated with (9) ....

There was nothing furtive in what I did. I knew my parents would see what I'd
done, and I didn't think there was any (10) .... in it. They always let me
(11) .... the corners after they'd opened them. Why should I think there was
any harm in doing it first, (12) .... in mind that they weren't on hand to be
(13) .... Wouldn't they rather be left to doze in their summer deckchairs?

(14) .... , though, my father solemnly showed me his letters. They looked
distinctly moth-eaten, with bites taken out of the corners and sides. I began to
(15) .... what I'd done!

1	**A** stare	**B** watch	**C** look	**D** peer
2	**A** glad	**B** pleased	**C** eager	**D** excited
3	**A** came	**B** was	**C** lay	**D** arrived
4	**A** investigate	**B** observe	**C** see	**D** notice
5	**A** junior	**B** tender	**C** small	**D** little
6	**A** struck	**B** seemed	**C** appeared	**D** felt
7	**A** nearby	**B** close	**C** next	**D** round
8	**A** able	**B** possibly	**C** possible	**D** could
9	**A** gentleness	**B** caution	**C** honour	**D** respect
10	**A** trouble	**B** wrong	**C** bad	**D** harm
11	**A** take	**B** tear	**C** cut	**D** remove
12	**A** having	**B** holding	**C** bearing	**D** keeping
13	**A** consulted	**B** advised	**C** queried	**D** requested
14	**A** After	**B** Then	**C** Later	**D** Soon
15	**A** accept	**B** realize	**C** admit	**D** confess

PART 2

For questions 16–30, read the text below and think of the word which best fits each space. Use only one word in each space.

An amazing character

Have you read *The Tin Drum* by Günter Grass? If not, you should get a copy and read it as soon as (16) .... It's an amazing novel with an amazing main character. This character, Oskar, has the (17) .... to destroy things at a distance, (18) .... by screaming. With his piercing scream he can even shatter the super-tough (19) .... in jewellers' windows, and this leads to quite a (20) .... of thefts.

The novel is (21) .... of memorable episodes and has been made into a very successful film. (22) .... out for it in your local cinema! But (23) .... all, borrow or buy a copy of the novel itself. It's available in paperback so you shouldn't (24) .... it too expensive. Once you've read it the sound of that scream (25) .... echo round your head for the (26) .... of your life.

It may seem strange, but a well-written novel has far more effect on you than a film. Perhaps it's (27) .... you have to use your imagination when you're reading, whereas a film-maker (28) .... the imagining for you. Compare *The Tin Drum* as book and film and you'll see what I (29) ....

Having read the novel, I can't get Oskar and that dreadful scream of his out of my head! No (30) .... I've got a headache again!

Before you check your answers, go on to page 76.

FILL IN THE MISSING WORD

Look again at questions 16–30 on page 75 and choose which of the four options below best fits each gap. You may wish to change some of your answers to the test after you have done this. However, an answer in the test is not necessarily wrong just because it is not among the choices here.

16 **A** possible   **B** ever   **C** earliest   **D** once   ☐

17 **A** means   **B** ability   **C** strength   **D** influence   ☐

18 **A** only   **B** easily   **C** just   **D** even   ☐

19 **A** glass   **B** shutters **C** security   **D** panes   ☐

20 **A** load   **B** number   **C** crime   **D** rise   ☐

21 **A** made   **B** full   **C** consisting   **D** comprised   ☐

22 **A** Go   **B** See   **C** Watch   **D** Make   ☐

23 **A** over   **B** above   **C** beyond   **D** after   ☐

24 **A** discover   **B** have   **C** find   **D** meet   ☐

25 **A** must   **B** makes   **C** will   **D** shall   ☐

26 **A** rest   **B** whole   **C** time   **D** days   ☐

27 **A** because   **B** therefore **C** why   **D** that   ☐

28 **A** makes   **B** does   **C** achieves   **D** performs   ☐

29 **A** say   **B** mean   **C** tell   **D** describe   ☐

30 **A** surprise   **B** use   **C** doubt   **D** wonder   ☐

Now check your answers to Part 2.

PART 3

For questions 31–40, complete the second sentence so that it has a similar meaning to the first sentence, using the word given. **Do not change the word given**. You must use between two and five words, including the word given.

31   You should telephone her.
speak
You should .... on the telephone.

32   My house is near to John's.
close
John .... each other.

33   I gave her my address.
where
I .... lived.

34   Your brakes are faulty.
wrong
There's .... brakes.

35   He took two hours deciding which seeds to buy.
mind
He took two hours .... which seeds to buy.

36   After the storm the repairs to my house cost me £200.
have
It cost me £200 .... after the storm.

37   The population of Spain is increasing.
people
The .... is increasing.

38   The train is due now.
time
It .... arrived.

39   You should join the football club.
member
You should .... the football club.

40   I didn't expect to win.
think
I .... win.

PART 4

For questions 41–55, read the text below and look carefully at each line. Some of the lines are correct and some have a word that should not be there.
If a line is correct, put a tick (✓) by the number. If a line has a word which should **not** be there, write the word down.

City pollution

.... 41 Since the introduction of the motor car at the beginning of

.... 42 this century, our roads have become more and more congested

.... 43 and our cities has increasingly polluted. In Mexico City,

.... 44 for example, where there are over two million of

.... 45 cars, children are quite used to smog alerts. It is said that

.... 46 the damage being caused to children's lungs is the same as that

.... 47 from smoking the two packets of cigarettes a day.

.... 48 Seen from up the air, cities such as London and Los Angeles

.... 49 appear to be covered in a blanket of cloud that is, in a fact,

.... 50 the haze of pollution. Car manufacturers and city planners are

.... 51 now hard working to try and control the number of vehicles and

.... 52 improve the way they run to make them less bad polluting. One

.... 53 major advance forward has been the development of the electric

.... 54 car. Using batteries, these vehicles are able to move quietly

.... 55 around cities creating very little of pollution.

PART 5

For questions 56–65, read the text below. Use the word given in capitals at the end of each line to form a word that fits in the space in the same line.

The ideal speech

Giving the ideal speech is a matter of (56) .... in yourself	CONFIDENT
and in what you're going to say. This may be (57) .... said	EASY
than done, but part of the answer lies in your careful (58)	PREPARE
Note down your key points, (59) .... on postcards or other	PREFER
small slips. Don't make the mistake of trying to script your	
speech word for word. You may gain a sense of (60) .... from	SECURE
doing this but when you come to deliver your speech it will	
sound (61)	NATURE
Keep it brief. It's no good saying afterwards, 'I delivered	
it well but they fell asleep.' To grab their (62) .... , begin	ATTEND
your speech with a few arresting thoughts or phrases, but	
steer clear of jokes. As a (63) .... , you'll show your	BEGIN
(64) .... in your face as you wonder whether your joke will	NERVOUS
succeed. Be a top-class speaker – not an amateur (65) .... !	COMEDY

Before you check your answers, go on to page 80.

FILL IN THE MISSING WORD

To help you to make sure you have the correct answers to questions 56–65 on page 79, complete the text below by using the words given in capitals to form words that fit in the spaces. Then compare your two sets of answers, which should have similar endings, for example, 56 and 66 both end in -ence (though be careful with 59 and 69!).

John showed great (66) .... in overcoming his injuries. As	PERSIST
soon as his hands grew (67) .... he decided to spend his	STEADY
(68) .... money on a horse-riding holiday. Unable to stand	COMPENSATE
for very long, he chose a train with (69) .... seats. Apart	RESERVE
from that he refused to fuss about his health – except for	
insisting on the absolute (70) .... of his drinking water.	PURE
When he went away he had several bottles of (71) .... spring	NATURE
water in his case. 'It's the best (72) .... since springs them-	INVENT
selves,' he said as he left. 'If you see me riding a (73) .... ,	WIN
it means I've got some of this stuff inside me,' he joked.	
His (74) .... is always the same, and I just hope he'll soon be	CHEERFUL
well enough to return to his work as a professional (75)	MUSIC

Now check your answers to these questions and reconsider your answers to Part 5 on page 79. Then check your answers to Part 5.

PAPER 4 LISTENING

PART 1

You will hear people talking in eight different situations.
For questions 1–8, choose the best answer A, B or C.

1 You overhear a customer complaining in a shop or garage.
   She is complaining about

   A a coat.
   B a car. | 1 |
   C a skirt.

2 You will hear someone speaking on the telephone to a taxi firm.
   He is going to

   A cancel his journey.
   B ring another taxi firm. | 2 |
   C just wait for a taxi to come and pick him up.

3 You will hear a dentist and his patient speaking to one another.
   The patient is going to have two teeth removed because

   A they're too bad to save.
   B he's tired of having them filled. | 3 |
   C he's in pain.

4 You will hear a mother who is pleased with the good report her son has just brought
   home from school.
   The most surprising improvement in Peter's work is in

   A geography.
   B maths. | 4 |
   C French.

5 You will hear a conversation between a child and the person who is teaching him to
   play the drums.
   The teacher wants his pupil to

   A play faster.
   B play more lightly. | 5 |
   C practise hitting the drums more sharply.

6 You will hear a man who is not very happy about a job which someone has offered him.
   His main concern is

   A the pay.
   B the chance of having his money stolen. | 6 |
   C the risks and responsibilities he would have to take.

7 You will hear a travel agent talking to someone who is booking airline tickets. His journey will finish in

    A Dresden.
    B Moscow.
    C Amsterdam.

	7

8 You will hear the start of a lecture about how people are affected by different colours. The lecturer thinks that blue is a bad colour for

    A national flags.
    B china and plates.
    C food.

	8

PART 2

You will hear part of a talk about antique collecting.
For questions 9–18, complete the notes which summarize what the speaker says. You will need to write a word or a short phrase in each box.

You'll soon have to stop collecting antiques if you		9

The best way to start is to go to local events including, for example,		10

and		11

To avoid wasting money and time the speaker made sure that he never had more than		12

People selling antiques are good at		13

You can quickly resell things that		14

Once you've sold them you can		15

Rather than seeking good quality things you should		16

However, with experience you can buy things like crystal vases and		17

You should make sure you have a suitable		18

PART 3

You will hear five different people talking about their hobbies.
For questions 19–23, choose from the list A–F what each one does. Use each letter only once. There is one extra letter which you do not need to use.

A   Gardening.   Speaker 1   **19**

B   Running.   Speaker 2   **20**

C   Model making.
                        Speaker 3   **21**

D   Cycling.
                        Speaker 4   **22**

E   Walking.

F   Sailing.   Speaker 5   **23**

PART 4

You will hear a conversation which takes place at a second-hand shop between a taxi driver, his passenger Jenny and the woman called Ann who runs the shop.

Answer questions 24–30 by writing   **T** (for taxi driver)
                                        J (for Jenny)
                                or   **A** (for Ann)   in the boxes provided.

24   Who isn't satisfied at first?   **24**

25   Who has made a recommendation?   **25**

26   Who holds the door open?   **26**

27   Who mentions someone called Philip?   **27**

28   Who thinks it's a good policy to help others?   **28**

29   Who comments on someone else's spending?   **29**

30   Who wants to go home?   **30**

A DETAILED STUDY

In many parts of the examination you will need to be aware of feelings and implications as well as facts. Listen again to Part 1 of the test on pages 81 and 82 and answer the following questions.

1   Which situation has a speaker who is

a   worried?

b   managing to stay patient, despite being provoked?

c   impressed and pleased?

d   frustrated at first, then impressed and pleased?

e   dismayed or alarmed?

f   irritated or fed up?

2   Now complete the following sentence.
Less feeling comes over in the remaining two situations because ....
....

3   Choose titles for each situation 1–8 from the following list A–I. (There is one extra title which you do not need to use.) You may be able to do this without listening to Part 1 again. If you can't remember the numbers, refer to the situations with brief descriptions (eg 'the passage with the man at the dentist').

A   Food for thought.

B   Excellent service.

C   Success at last.

D   Down in the mouth.

E   Solving a problem.

F   Paying for someone else's crime.

G   One thing at a time.

H   Timing it right.

I   Not again!

PAPER 5 SPEAKING

PART 1

Answer these questions about yourself.

How do you feel about the number of leisure facilities in your town/city?
Which appeals to you most? What do you like about it?
What about holidays? Where do you go and what do you do?
What's the best holiday you've ever had?

PART 2

Look at the photographs on page 121 and answer one of the following questions. Then answer a different question about the photographs on page 122.

What's happening in each photograph? Would you like to be involved?
Which sort of holiday would you prefer? Why?
Which sort of holiday activity would you recommend for your partner or friend? Why?

PART 3

Look at the maps and answer the questions which follow them.

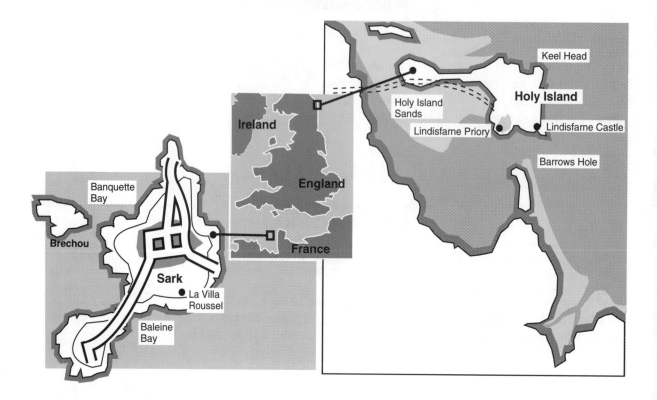

Which of the two islands would you rather spend a brief holiday on? Why?
What would you do?
What sort of person do you think would get most out of staying on the island? Why?

For Further Practice and Guidance, see page 87.

PART 4

Answer these questions.

How do tourists spoil popular spots? What can be done about it?
Holidays can sometimes be a strain. What sort of things commonly go wrong and how can people guard against them?
What sort of holiday could you organize for someone in your own locality?
What do you think people mean when they say a change is as good as a rest? Do you think it's true and if so why?

WORKING THINGS OUT WITH PICTURES

In Part 3 of Paper 5, you and your partner will have to reach a decision or work something out using one or more pictures or diagrams. The examiner will be interested in your reasoning as well as your conclusion so speak to your partner clearly – in English, of course!

For practice, work out the story told in these five pictures. Say what has happened to the football boots and explain how you know.

Remember: There probably won't be any 'right' answers in Paper 5. It won't matter what you decide as long as you tackle the task in a sensible way and explain yourself clearly.

TEST FOUR

PAPER 1 READING

You are going to read a magazine article about planning for holidays. Choose the most suitable heading from the list A–H for each part (1–7) of the article. There is one extra heading which you do not need to use.

A The price of success.

B Prevention is better than cure.

C Be prepared for the worst.

D Stranded!

E An unwelcome visitor!

F No room at the inn!

G The price of forgetfulness.

H An empty cupboard?

Plan it Beforehand!

1

Organizing a holiday isn't the easiest task in the world; there are so many things to think about. Let's keep it simple – well, relatively simple – by assuming that there's no overseas travel to
5 arrange. Does that mean that you can also forget about injections and other health precautions entirely? Not a bit of it! What about sun blocker? What about regular medication prescribed by your doctor? My point, quite frankly, is that
10 planning a holiday can be a real pain – though a well-planned holiday can more than reward the pains you go to before you set out.

2

Talking of pains, where do you go if you're taken ill away from home? It sounds pessimistic to talk
15 like this but it's unwise to leave a decision until you're too ill to make one! So find out, before you go away, all addresses and telephone numbers you might need if disaster strikes.

3

Don't forget that your vehicle, if you have one,
20 may well need urgent attention in a lay-by many miles from home. Of course, you don't know exactly where a breakdown will happen but you do know which counties you'll be driving through. If you're a member of a motoring
25 organization, find out the emergency number appropriate to each county – and have it on you.

4

So far we haven't mentioned accommodation but you'll obviously need it. If part of the fun of a holiday is to turn up somewhere and then look
30 for 'digs', that's all very well. You're presumably happy to risk a 'no vacancy' situation, even if that means spending a restless night in your car or beneath a hedge. And for you that may be the best fun of all!

5

Such holiday tastes, though fascinating, are far 35
from normal. For most of us, being moved on unexpectedly at two in the morning is far from enjoyable – especially if the disturbance comes from an irritable bull snorting at us and nudging us with its fearsome horns. It's the price we'll 40
sometimes have to pay if we decide we can't be bothered to make a prior booking at a proper campsite, and striking camp in the dark, harassed by horns and with nowhere to go, is not a joke. 45

6

As well as arranging accommodation – or at least an official patch of ground – you may need to fix some advance supplies. If you turn up at your self-catering flat at six o'clock on a Saturday evening, you may have to wait till 50
Monday morning before you can find an open shop. No one wants a hungry start to a holiday and whoever lets the accommodation may well be willing to purchase some basic groceries on your behalf, and even arrange for milk and 55
newspapers to be delivered.

7

Milk and newspapers! Have you remembered to cancel deliveries at your normal address? Is your home insured against burglary? Are you insured against your holiday being cancelled or curtailed 60
due to some emergency? Well, if you're already on holiday, you may as well stop worrying and do your best to enjoy yourself. Oh, but have you remembered your cheque book or your credit cards? Without them you'll have to sing in the 65
streets to pay for your food and your journey home. In the end, the most easy-going of people can wish they'd done a little planning!

PART 2

You are going to read the start of a book called *My Early Life* by Sir Winston Churchill, who was once the British Prime Minister. For questions 8–14, choose the answer (A, B, C or D) which you think fits best according to the text.

Various accounts have appeared from time to time of my early life and adventures, and I myself having published thirty years ago stories of the several campaigns in which I took part, and having written later about particular episodes, I have thought it right to bring the whole together in a single
5 complete story; and to tell the tale, such as it is, anew. I have therefore not only searched my memory, but I have most carefully verified my facts from the records which I possess. I have tried, in each part of the quarter-century in which this tale lies, to show the point of view appropriate to my years, whether as a child, a schoolboy, a cadet, a subaltern, a war-correspondent or a youthful politician. If these
10 opinions conflict with those now generally accepted they must be taken merely as representing a phase in my early life and not in any respect, except where the context warrants, as modern pronouncements.

When I survey this work as a whole I find I have drawn a picture of a vanished age. The character of society, the foundations of politics, the methods of war, the outlook
15 of youth, the scale of values, all are changed, and changed to an extent I should not have believed possible in so short a space without any violent domestic revolution. I cannot pretend to think that they are in all respects changed for the better. I was a child in the Victorian era, when the structure of our country seemed firmly set. In those days, the dominant forces in Great Britain were very sure of themselves and of
20 their doctrines. They thought they could teach the world the art of government and the science of economics. They were sure they were supreme at sea and consequently safe at home. They rested therefore sedately under the convictions of power and security. Very different is the aspect of these anxious and dubious times. Full allowance for such changes should be made by friendly readers.

25 I have thought that it might be of interest to the new generation to read a story of youthful endeavour, and I have set down candidly and with as much simplicity as possible my personal fortunes as far as I could remember them.

When does one first begin to remember? When do the wavering lights and shadows of dawning consciousness cast their print upon the mind of a child? My earliest
30 memories are set in Ireland. I can recall scenes and events in Ireland quite well; and sometimes, dimly, even people. Yet I was born on November 30, 1874, and I left Ireland early in the year 1879. I nonetheless have clear and vivid impressions of some events. For example, I remember an occasion when we were to go to a pantomime. There was great excitement about it. We started from our official
35 residence and drove to a castle, where other children were no doubt to be picked up. Inside the castle was a great square space paved, I remember, with small oblong stones. It rained. It nearly always rained – just as it does now. People came out of the door of the castle, and there seemed to be much stir. It turned out that we could not go to the pantomime because the theatre had burned down. All that was found of
40 the manager was the keys that had been in his pocket.

We were promised as a consolation for not going to the pantomime to go next day and see the ruins of the building. I wanted very much to see the keys but this request does not seem to have been well received.

8   Churchill says he is writing the book to

    A   bring the account up to date.
    B   collect everything together in one book.
    C   get facts correct.
    D   make the story sound fresh and new.

9   The book mostly shows

    A   what Churchill thought at the time things happened.
    B   Churchill's views at the time he wrote it.
    C   the views that are generally accepted.
    D   the latest ideas, where these fit into the book as a whole.

10   The second paragraph refers to a change

    A   in family life.
    B   from stability to instability.
    C   from Britain being a confident nation to a nervous one.
    D   from Britain being well defended to being at risk of attack.

11   Churchill thinks that readers may not appreciate his book unless they understand

    A   how attitudes have changed.
    B   that Churchill now feels worried and unsure of himself.
    C   why opinions in the book may differ from theirs.
    D   that some things are told from a child's or young person's point of view.

12   Churchill is struck by the fact that his first memories

    A   date from when he was very young.
    B   throw light on a child's first thoughts and ideas.
    C   are so clear and vivid.
    D   are often of ordinary people and things.

13   Judging by the first paragraph of the passage, the statement 'all that was found of the manager was the keys that had been in his pocket' is likely to be

    A   true.
    B   a story the children made up.
    C   a story the adults made up.
    D   something Churchill read later.

14   It seems from the passage that Churchill grew up in

    A   a poor family.
    B   a family that owned a lot of land.
    C   a military family.
    D   a family that had an important role in government.

Before you check your answers, go on to pages 92 and 93.

A DETAILED STUDY

The questions below will help you to make sure that you have chosen the correct options for questions 8–14 on pages 90 and 91.

Questions 8 and 9 Look at the first paragraph of the text and answer this question.
Which of the following quotations gives the answer to question 8 in the text and which gives the answer to question 9?

a   I have thought it right to bring the whole together in a single complete story.
b   I have most carefully verified my facts from the records which I possess.
c   If these opinions conflict with those now generally accepted they must be taken merely as representing a phase in my early life and not in any respect, except where the context warrants, as modern pronouncements.

....

....

Question 10 Look at the second paragraph and answer this question.
Two consecutive sentences (towards the end of the paragraph) support one of the options A–D. Which option is it? (If you find this hard, work out who is meant by 'they'.)

....

....

Question 11 Look at the second paragraph and answer these questions.
1   Churchill's remark about friendly readers comes at the end of this paragraph. Which of the options A–D refer to the first paragraph and which to the second paragraph?

....

....

2   Which paragraph is likely to give you the answer to the question in the test?

....

....

Question 12 Look at the fourth paragraph and answer this question.
Which of the options A–D is suggested by the words 'I was born on November 30, 1874, and I left Ireland early in the year 1879'?

....

....

Question 13 Look at the whole passage and answer these questions.

1   Which statement in the first paragraph helps you to choose between options A–D?

....

....

2   In which part of the passage do you find the shortest sentences and how does this help to
confirm your chosen option?

....

....

Question 14 Look at the fourth paragraph and answer this question.
One clue to the sort of family Churchill grew up in is that they lived in an 'official residence'.
Assuming that this is the only clue, put options A–D in order of probability.

....

....

Now check your answers to these questions and reconsider your answers to Part 2 on pages
90 and 91. Then check your answers to Part 2.

FURTHER PRACTICE AND GUIDANCE

PART 3

You are going to read part of the introduction to a book about very unusual words. Seven sentences have been removed from the passage. Choose from the sentences A–H the one which fits each gap (15–21). There is one extra sentence that you do not need to use.

I have called this book *The Insomniac's Dictionary* partly because it was born in the dark hours of night during my own periods of sleeplessness. | **15** | For one thing, it
5 doesn't require much in the way of mental or emotional commitment. And secondly, it's not meant to be read through at once. I encourage everyone to skim and skip around a bit.

The Insomniac's Dictionary presents nearly 3,000
10 strange and intriguing words, all of which are grouped together by categories. | **16** | It's been more than a dozen years since I first discovered the joys of dictionary reading. From the very beginning, I was amazed by the
15 richness of our language. I quickly became enchanted with words like kakistocracy (government by the worst citizens), and I wanted more. | **17** | It didn't take long to realize I was stymied – there were books that
20 included these delightful words but none that grouped them together to be enjoyed as a whole. | **18** |

The results are here for you to enjoy. Some of the thematic lists are as all-inclusive as I could
25 make them. Every chapter has been thoroughly and painstakingly researched. I cannot claim that the resulting lists are absolutely complete

but can state that they are more complete than any lists that can be found in any other reference books.   30

| **19** | Such chapters are intended merely as introductions to their respective subjects. By way of example, our language contains over 20,000 eponyms (words which are based on a person's name). Most of these are obscure   35
scientific terms or measurements and it's obviously beyond the scope of this book to list them all. | **20** |

Most of the word lists are pretty long, and I've therefore chosen to divide them into smaller   40
groups. I admit these sub-categories are totally arbitrary – they are a means of presenting the words in easier-to-digest servings and should not be construed as definitive classification. | **21** | Remember, this book is best   45
enjoyed by browsing, not straightforward reading.

A Thus my research began.
B And speaking of digestibility, I would not recommend reading some of the longer chapters at one sitting.
C It wouldn't be much fun either.
D On the other hand, some of the chapters make no attempt to be all-inclusive.
E More to the point, it's the perfect book for insomniacs, book browsers and anyone else with a little time to while away.
F By way of explaining why I've chosen this format, I'd like to briefly relate my inspiration for writing this book.
G I wanted to see all the weird and wonderful words there were.
H Though it may be hard to believe, all entries in *The Insomniac's Dictionary* are real words.

PART 4

You are going to read some information about bikes for touring.
For questions 22–35, choose from the bikes (A–E). Some of the bikes may be chosen more than once. When more than one answer is required, these may be given in any order.

According to the information given, which of the bikes

is relatively inexpensive to buy?	22	
is inexpensive to run?	23	
copes well with rough ground?	24	
is relatively difficult to ride safely?	25	
is hard work at times?	26	
is assisted by an electric motor?	27	
are sturdy?	28	29
are good for going uphill?	30	31
are attractive to thieves?	32	33
are fast?	34	35

Choosing two wheels

Mountain bikes   A

For the young couple planning a holiday on two wheels there are various transport options to choose from. Let's start with the cheapest – the mountain bike (or rather a pair of mountain bikes, since they'll need one each). Mountain bikes are strong, resilient machines, capable of bouncing down rocky paths without suffering any ill effects. (The riders may suffer some ill effects from their bruising ride, but that's another matter.) Modern mountain bikes have a good range of gears – often as many as 12 or 15 – so getting to the top in the first place shouldn't prove too difficult.

'Bikes with a boost'   B

There's a new invention that provides an even easier solution to steep ascents: the 'booster' device which can be permanently fixed to a bicycle and engaged or disengaged according to the state of the terrain (though the attachment can be more trouble than it's worth if riding cross-country). At the flick of a switch the 'booster' comes into operation, gently helping to propel the rear wheel when uphill stretches present themselves. Once over the hump, the cyclist flicks the switch again and the drive detaches itself from the wheel. The power pack recharges overnight at a cost of only a penny or two. The gadget itself costs over a hundred pounds to buy and unfortunately makes the bike an expensive travel option – and also quite a prize for those with light fingers.

Racing cycles   C

Returning to unaided pedal power as the motive force, it's worthwhile for the intending holiday-makers to consider racing cycles. Whereas mountain bikes have sturdy frames and wide wheels offering excellent grip and safety, even on loose surfaces, a racing cycle has a light-weight frame and narrow wheels. The contact with the road or track is that much less and the route and manner of cycling need adjusting with regard to safety. Rough terrain must be avoided; on the other hand, the racing cycle offers ease and speed, so a greater distance can be covered in a day and a bigger range of scenery can be enjoyed, though not necessarily at the closest quarters.

Traditional tandems   D

Another option when it comes to unaided pedal power is the traditional tandem – the bicycle made for two. A tandem is a heavy machine – just a little too 'chunky' for some people's liking. They are rarely found in racing varieties – and are far more wasteful of effort than they need to be. Having said this, it is of course a great energy-saver in that only one machine is involved instead of two. A drawback is its lack of flexibility: if either rider wants to stay put – say erecting a tent – while the other wants to go for supplies, it's hardly worthwhile to ride the tandem. It can be ridden by only one but the effort involved is almost as great as the effort of walking and the machine will probably need to be wheeled up any hills. On such occasions the holiday-makers will wish that they had two bikes after all.

Motor bikes   E

Our final option is a petrol driven 'ton-up' bike – a machine which carries one or two with equal ease. Speed is maximized and so is noise – a feature which may appeal to some young folk, but not if they wish to converse or enjoy the song of the birds. They won't even be able to enjoy the feel of the wind in their hair, since the compulsory helmet will enclose their heads in unwelcome casing. There are other legal requirements too, including a licence, insurance and a good pair of tyres. These all cost money and so does fuel. A watch will need to be kept for any envious eyes whenever the bike is parked for the night – or while the riders take a meal.

Before you check your answers, go on to pages 97 and 98.

A DETAILED STUDY

The questions below will help you to make sure that you have chosen the correct options for questions 22–35 on pages 95 and 96.

Questions 22 and 23 Look at the text and answer this question.
Find the following quotations and make sure you understand them properly. Which two give the answers to the questions in the test?

a Let's start with the cheapest.

b The gadget itself costs over a hundred pounds to buy and unfortunately makes the bike an expensive travel option.

c The power pack recharges overnight at a cost of only a penny or two.

d … a licence, insurance and a good pair of tyres … all cost money and so does fuel.

....

....

Question 24 Look at the text and answer this question.
Which two paragraphs give you the answer (or good clues) to the question in the test?

....

....

Question 25 Look at the text and answer this question.
Which paragraph says 'rough terrain must be avoided' and what reason does it suggest for this?

....

....

Question 26 Look at the text and answer this question.
Paragraph D says that a tandem is 'a great energy-saver' but it also refers to 'the effort involved'. How can you explain this apparent contradiction?

....

....

Question 27 Look at the text and answer this question.
What does 'assisted' mean and what clue can you find that one bike has an electric motor and is not powered in some other way?

....

....

Questions 28 and 29 Look at the text and answer this question.
Which adjectives in the passage suggest sturdiness and which bikes do they describe?

....

....

Questions 30 and 31 Look at the text and answer this question.
Which bike has 'a good range of gears' and which has 'a "booster" device'?

....

....

Questions 32 and 33 Look at the text and answer this question.
We can refer to good gardeners as people with green fingers and the passage uses similar
expressions to refer to thieves. What are they?

....

....

Questions 34 and 35 Look at the text and answer this question.
Which two paragraphs refer to 'speed'?

....

....

Advice: If you have to guess, by all means use your common sense and general knowledge
but first do your best to base your answers on the information you are given. Common
sense and general knowledge suggest that a motor bike (E) is a fast two-wheeled vehicle, so
you may be tempted to give E as one of your answers to questions 34 and 35. However, you
need to check what, if anything, the passage says about a motor bike's speed. Remember
you're being asked about the passage, not tested on your general knowledge.

Now check your answers to these questions and reconsider your answers to Part 4 on pages
95 and 96. Then check your answers to Part 4.

PAPER 2 WRITING

PART 1

Answer this question.

1 You are planning a summer holiday and you decide to reply to the advertisement shown below.

Carefully read the advertisement and the notes you have made. Then write your letter to the holiday company, covering the points in your notes and any other relevant points.

Write a letter of between 120 and 180 words in an appropriate style. Do not include addresses.

Riding hats etc. provided?

Horse Riding Holidays

Everyone catered for, from novice to advanced.
Treks through beautiful countryside, from 3 miles to 30 miles, from a long weekend to a fortnight or more.
Accommodation arranged - no worries.
Prices from £30 a day.

But what about absolute beginners?

Same place every night or what?

Vegetarian food?

Does this include the accommodation?

PART 2

Write an answer to one of the questions 2–5 in this part. Write your answer in 120–180 words in an appropriate style.

2 Write a short story beginning or ending with the words:
Jimmy showed me his finger, which was heavily bandaged.

3 Write a letter explaining how you think your local library or bus service could be improved. Begin with the words 'Dear Librarian' or 'Dear Transport Manager'. Do not include addresses.

4 Write an article describing an interesting hobby for people who know very little about it.

5 **Background reading texts**
Choose one of your set books and refer to various incidents to show which character changes or learns most in the course of the action.

Before you write your answers, go on to pages 100 and 101.

PLANNING A STORY

Question 2 on page 99 invites you to write a short story beginning or ending with the words 'Jimmy showed me his finger, which was heavily bandaged'. One of the secrets of writing a story is not to give everything away at once.

Below are two ways to continue a story starting with the words above. Tick the one which is better because it tells you less – and increases your interest.

a   'How did you do that?' I asked.
       'Come with me and I'll show you,' he replied.

b   'I did it yesterday, opening a tin,' he explained.

Pretend that someone has continued their story with **b** and then wants to puzzle or interest the reader. Tick the best two of the following ways of carrying on.

c   'But you told me you'd bought a new opener.
       You said it was a safe electric one.'

d   'Your Mum told me all about it,' I answered.

e   'Did it hurt when you did it?'

f   'Oh, yes!' I replied. 'I heard a scream – and then a
       noise like a gun going off. So what went wrong?'

Look again at **a** and **b** and add one or two sentences of your own to continue each of them in an interesting way.

....

....

....

....

Remember that if you write a story in the examination it should not be more than 120–180 words in length. That means that it cannot be full of varied incidents; one simple idea is all you need and then you should concentrate on filling it out with interesting description and/or dialogue.

Be clear about the central idea of your story before you start. Perhaps Jimmy says he'll show you how he injured his finger; you go along to see and you laugh at his stupidity, imitating his mistake – and injuring your own finger in the same way!

Plan two or three stories based on the sentence in the question (**a–f** above might help to give you ideas). If you write your story plans down, you should only need 15–25 words for each one. Once you have a choice of plans, pick your favourite and write the story out in full.

Advice: If you don't think you're good at writing interesting stories, don't worry too much. If your work is clear and well written you could get a high mark – and keeping it simple will help you in this.

FURTHER PRACTICE AND GUIDANCE

A SAMPLE ANSWER

Now read the following sample answer to question 2 on page 99. When you have read it, answer the questions which follow it, giving examples to back up what you say.

> In Summer of 1990 my group of friend went to Alpel of camping. we wanted to spend a week in the mountains but ours holiday were not as we had planned
>
> We were 6 ~~peps~~ people and slept 3 people in each tents. Edu, Jaime and Yimmy slept in a tent and Yoly, Betar and me slept in another tent. In the mornings we walk through the mountains. The boys used to climb some mountains while the girls swam in the lake or suntaned. the weather was so good that we can see some kinds of animals, reptil and insdects.
>
> One night yimmin saw a huracane that it came toward us! We ran a lot of but Yimmy fell and broke the bone of his finger. Jaime picked him up. we arrived at a village. The Next Day we went to camping and the tents had diseappeared all our things weren't There.
>
> We were laughed about our experrency and Jimmy showed me his finger, which was heavily bandaged and he told me: "It is the result of our holiday"

1   Does the story answer the question properly? Are there any parts which don't have much to do with how Jimmy's finger got injured?
2   Is the story arranged and paragraphed in an appropriate way?
3   Are the sentence structures correct and interesting? Are the sentences linked to one another to make the story flow smoothly and clearly?
4   Is there a good range of vocabulary and is it used correctly?
5   Are the verbs and nouns used grammatically? Are there any other points of grammar that need to be changed or improved?
6   Is the style appropriate?

Now check your assessment of this sample answer.

PAPER 3 USE OF ENGLISH

PART 1

For questions 1–15, read the text below and decide which word A, B, C or D best fits each space.

Norfolk - the ideal holiday playground

This article is the work of someone born and (1) .... up in Norfolk. It is not impartial. On the (2) .... , I'm near to being a fanatic about the county and all it has to (3) .... If you want to consider other holiday destinations, you are best advised to go (4) .... for your information.

So why am I so incredibly keen on my native county? Firstly, it's clean. This stems from the fact that the population is very (5) .... – less than half the average for an English county. (6) .... there are fewer people, there are fewer chimneys, fewer towns and fewer cars. And whereas other rural counties have motorways (7) .... through them, Norfolk – largely bounded by sea – has very (8) .... through traffic whatsoever, and not an inch of motorway.

Norfolk offers a hundred miles of beautiful inland waterways and, in (9) .... , a hundred miles of unspoilt coastal scenery. (10) .... the coast there are nature reserves (11) .... seals, rare birds and other wildlife thrive in profusion. Long distance footpaths (12) .... almost the whole of this coast and people wander slowly along them peering (13) .... binoculars. This is quite an amusing sight, though one sometimes (14) .... for their safety near to the edge of the cliffs!

If you're feeling (15) .... , Norfolk is the place for you!

1	**A** brought	**B** raised	**C** reared	**D** grown
2	**A** opposite	**B** whole	**C** evidence	**D** contrary
3	**A** praise	**B** provide	**C** offer	**D** give
4	**A** elsewhere	**B** away	**C** off	**D** there
5	**A** slight	**B** thin	**C** low	**D** little
6	**A** Whereas	**B** Because	**C** Although	**D** While
7	**A** driving	**B** running	**C** leading	**D** dividing
8	**A** few	**B** little	**C** slight	**D** scarce
9	**A** addition	**B** fact	**C** reality	**D** places
10	**A** With	**B** Next	**C** Beside	**D** Along
11	**A** where	**B** with	**C** that	**D** while
12	**A** along	**B** accompany	**C** follow	**D** run
13	**A** with	**B** into	**C** through	**D** by
14	**A** worries	**B** dreads	**C** fears	**D** wonders
15	**A** lowly	**B** worn	**C** weary	**D** heavy

Before you check your answers, go on to page 103.

WORK IT OUT

In questions like 1–15 on page 102, you will sometimes find it hard to decide which word to choose. Keep calm! The chances are that you've already met the suggested words in other contexts, so your mind is stocked with examples of the way they're used. Take your eyes off the text and try to remember – or make up – examples for each of the words. If you invent sample sentences for Question 1 like the ones below, for example, you will probably find that 'raised' and 'reared' aren't followed by 'up'.

A   He brought up the matter of the unpaid bill.
B   He raised his family on a very low wage.
C   She reared chickens and ducks on her farm.
D   All her family are grown up now.

You may well find that the presence of 'up' restricts your choice to A ('brought') and D ('grown'). If so, it's time to think about how the passage uses 'was'. Would we say 'he was brought up by his parents' or 'he was grown up by his parents'? In other words, which word goes better in a passive construction like the one in the passage?

Question 2 gives the same sort of challenge. Try using each of the four suggested words to form a phrase with 'on the' at the start of a sentence. (Note the comma which marks off the three-word phrase from the rest.) You may finish up with two or three phrases that seem to 'work' in your sample sentences. If so, think about the sentences that might come before them. What sort of link do the phrases make? Is it the same sort of link as the one in the printed passage?

Another way of approaching any 'difficult' gaps is to decide on your own way of filling the gap, even if it means making changes to the text. For example, for Question 9 you could probably change the passage to 'Norfolk offers a hundred miles of beautiful inland waterways and (it) also (offers) a hundred miles of unspoilt coastal scenery'.

In some cases, doing this will lead you directly to one of the four suggested words. Here, however, 'also' is not in the list (and you couldn't use it after 'in') so you have to ask yourself which of the given words forms a phrase with a similar meaning to 'also'. Working like this can be particularly useful when a missing word links two sentences or parts of a sentence.

Advice: Always consider the passage carefully and think about alternative versions.

Now reconsider your answers to Part 1 on page 102. Then check your answers to Part 1.

PART 2

For questions 16–30, read the text below and think of the word which best fits each space. Use only one word in each space.

Mary the menace

As I shot round the corner on my bicycle I saw Mary coming the other way. Unfortunately, she was (16) .... the wrong side of the road and a collision seemed inevitable.

There was a split second in (17) .... I saw Mary's fingers move on her handlebars; I suppose she must have been using her brakes (18) .... a hopeless effort to stop (19) .... time. There was another split second in which I saw her leaning her body outwards, (20) .... from the point of impact.

And then it happened. I remember the clang (21) .... our bicycles locked in a moment of combat. I don't remember flying (22) .... the air, though I (23) .... remember the moment of take-off, when I suddenly had (24) .... saddle beneath me. I also remember the moment of landing and Mary's voice (25) .... , 'Are you all right?'

I was quite impressed to hear her expressing concern for me (26) .... the very moment her bicycle frame was coming down over her (27) .... and shoulders. She looked like a prize on a hooplah stall.

Well, was I all right? I was angry (28) .... having been knocked off my bike and deposited in the gutter, but I was humbled too – humbled by the way she put others (29) .... , even in a moment of crisis and pain. 'Oh fine, thanks,' I (30) .... 'Are you OK?'

PART 3

For questions 31–40, complete the second sentence so that it has a similar meaning to the first sentence, using the word given. **Do not change the word given**. You must use between two and five words, including the word given.

31 I can't move until I've sold my house.
   unable
   Until I've sold my house .... move.

32 My parcel hasn't arrived yet.
   received
   I still .... my parcel.

33 After this, I won't give you any more warnings.
   last
   This is .... give you.

34 The dry weather is killing all the plants in my garden.
   dying
   All the plants in my garden .... the dry weather.

35 The mouse frightened him.
   scared
   He .... the mouse.

36 He couldn't stop quickly enough to avoid the accident.
   time
   He couldn't .... the accident.

37 It looked as if the carrots were bad.
   appeared
   The carrots .... bad.

38 I was lost so I asked the way.
   because
   I .... I was lost.

39 I'm hungry enough to eat two lunches.
   so
   I'm .... two lunches.

40 The return fare is double the single fare.
   twice
   The return fare .... the single fare.

Before you check your answers, go on to page 106.

COMPLETE THE SENTENCES

This page will help you to check your answers to questions 31–40 on page 105. Each sentence has been partly completed, with the word you must use in its correct position. Add the rest of the missing word(s).

31 I can't move until I've sold my house.
Until I've sold my house .... unable .... move.

32 My parcel hasn't arrived yet.
I still .... received my parcel.

33 After this, I won't give you any more warnings.
This is .... last .... give you.

34 The dry weather is killing all the plants in my garden.
All the plants in my garden .... dying .... the dry weather.

35 The mouse frightened him.
He .... scared .... the mouse.

36 He couldn't stop quickly enough to avoid the accident.
He couldn't .... time .... the accident.

37 It looked as if the carrots were bad.
The carrots appeared .... bad.

38 I was lost so I asked the way.
I .... because I was lost.

39 I'm hungry enough to eat two lunches.
I'm so .... two lunches.

40 The return fare is double the single fare.
The return fare .... twice the single fare.

Now check your answers to Part 3.

PART 4

For questions 41–55, read the text below and look carefully at each line. Some of the lines are correct and some have a word that should not be there.
If a line is correct, put a tick (✓) by the number. If a line has a word which should **not** be there, write the word down.

Preserving flowers

.... 41   Flowers picked in high summer and leaves gathered in the

.... 42   autumn can be pressed and used to make beautiful designs,

.... 43   while larger the flowers and sprays of leaves can be preserved

.... 44   in an almost natural state by drying them, which is best be

.... 45   done in the open air. Bunches of dried flowers make really

.... 46   beautiful winter decorations and will sometimes last you for

.... 47   years on end. Small, individual dried flowers can also be used up

.... 48   to make lovely designs on greetings cards. There is nothing to

.... 49   match the appeal of a card of which the sender has made by hand.

.... 50   It shows care and affection in such a way that a bought card can't

.... 51   possibly do so. If the flowers are carefully chosen for some

.... 52   personal meaning so much the better off. For example, primroses

.... 53   could be used to remind the recipient of a beautiful walk

.... 54   which you once shared together in woodland full of these

.... 55   beautiful flowers – which isn't to say why you should get the

flowers for your card from the wild.

PART 5

For questions 56–65, read the text below. Use the word given in capitals at the end of each line to form a word that fits in the space in the same line.

The key to good health

Healthy eating is (56) .... the key to general well-being.	DOUBT
Our bodies are made up of what we eat, so our (57) .... and	FIT
(58) .... cannot possibly escape the effects of bad diet.	VITAL
Sweets, chocolate and cake are fine in (59) .... , but trouble	MODERATE
arises when people just can't leave them alone, (60)	GREED
eating every possibly sticky item that comes their way. (61)	TREAT
is available for serious problems but (62) .... is normally	AVOID
better than cure. Make a careful (63) .... when it	CHOOSE
comes to desserts, and favour cafés that offer a good (64)	SELECT
of fruit to round off a meal. A (65) .... in your sugar intake	REDUCE
may well hurt at first but you'll feel better for it.	

Before you check your answers, go on to page 109.

WORK IT OUT

To answer questions 56–65 on page 108, you need to use affixes (parts added to the beginnings and ends of words) and when you add an affix to a word, you sometimes need to make a small adjustment to the word. For example, you may have to delete or change the last letter.

Below is a list of the changes which you should have made as you answered questions 56–65. The changes are not in order. Go through them and decide which of the affixes fits each word. You may wish to change some of your answers to the test after you have done this.

Delete the last letter and add -ion.

....

Add -ily.

....

Add un- and -edly.

....

Add -ness.

....

Add -ity.

....

Add -ment.

....

Add -ance.

....

Add -ion.

....

Delete the last letter and add -tion.

....

Change the last three letters to -ice.

....

Now check your answers to Part 5.

PAPER 4 LISTENING

PART 1

You will hear people talking in eight different situations.
For questions 1–8, choose the best answer A, B or C.

1   You overhear this conversation between a doctor and her patient, Mr Jones.
Mr Jones wants the doctor to

   A   give him some medicine.
   B   send him to hospital.
   C   examine him.

1

2   You will hear a dentist's receptionist talking to a patient, Mr Brownlow, on the phone.
The receptionist offers Mr Brownlow

   A   just an appointment for a thorough inspection.
   B   about six appointments.
   C   the chance to have all his treatment at once.

2

3   You will hear a woman and a man discussing Charlie, who has injured his leg.
Charlie is

   A   a cat.
   B   a dog.
   C   a child.

3

4   You will hear someone introducing some performers called The Bouncing Beans.
The Bouncing Beans are

   A   magicians.
   B   dancers.
   C   acrobats.

4

5   You will hear an angry market trader speaking to his supplier on the telephone.
The trader refuses

   A   an apology.
   B   a refund.
   C   a fresh delivery.

5

6   You will hear two people discussing a minor road accident.
According to these people, which vehicle was stationary when the accident happened?

   A   the bus or the lorry
   B   the van
   C   one of the cars

6

7 You will hear this announcement on a chat show.
Mr Cooke is famous as

A a singer.
B a violinist.
C a fashion designer.

| | 7 |

8 You will hear a couple – a woman called Alice and a man called Peter – who are going to a wedding reception together.
Alice suggests that if they buy some clothes beforehand they can

A put them in their car.
B take them to the reception in smart bags.
C wear them at the reception.

| | 8 |

PART 2

You will hear a woman called Jean telling you about her journeys to Birmingham.
For questions 9–18, complete the notes which summarize what she says. You will need to write a word or a short phrase in each box.

Jean lives in | 9 |

She has been studying leaflets about | 10 |

She is sure she doesn't want to travel by | 11 |

because she wouldn't like | 12 |

Last time she visited Birmingham she did the main part of the journey by | 13 |

which took about | 14 |

She was delayed on the way to Victoria because she | 15 |

She didn't let George know about this before leaving London because | 16 |

She thinks trains are better than coaches because they have | 17 |

This time she won't set off until she has | 18 |

PART 3

You will hear five different people talking about their experiences on holiday.
For questions 19–23, choose from the list A–F what happened to each one. Use each letter only once. There is one extra letter which you do not need to use.

A She/He travelled by bus or coach.	Speaker 1	**19**
B She/He went cycling.	Speaker 2	**20**
C Her/His train broke down.	Speaker 3	**21**
D Her/His catamaran or boat broke down.	Speaker 4	**22**
E She/He had a fast journey by car or train.	Speaker 5	**23**
F Her/His car needed attention.		

PART 4

You will hear a conversation in a shop between a customer, an assistant and the manager.

Answer questions 24–30 by writing   **C** (for customer)
                                        A (for assistant)
                        or   **M** (for manager)   in the boxes provided.

24   Who has to repeat something?   **24**

25   Who is 'a bit irritated'?   **25**

26   Who gives a firm assurance?   **26**

27   Who gives a warning?   **27**

28   Who cannot believe something?   **28**

29   Who is praised?   **29**

30   Who makes an apology?   **30**

A DETAILED STUDY

Listen again to Part 1 of the test on pages 110 and 111 and answer the following questions.

1 Look at the list of moods and attitudes A–G. In each case say which situation (1–8) displays this mood or attitude. One mood/attitude is found in <u>two</u> of the situations, so you will need to put <u>two</u> numbers in the box.

A Interested.

B Argumentative.

C Worked up and angry.

D Too talkative.

E Affectionate and concerned.

F Enthusiastic.

G Angry, then relieved and grateful.

2 The following sentences A–H could have come from the situations in Part 1. Say which situation each sentence could have come from. You may be able to do this without listening to Part 1 again. If you can't remember the numbers, refer to the situations with brief descriptions (eg 'the passage where the man is ringing the dentist').

A That's just what I need to keep me going.

B Here they are now, vibrant as ever.

C Well, let's add a face to the feast of sounds.

D No such luck for me – I'll have to go or I shall be late for work.

E We can't do that – it's completely impracticable.

F It just won't do to treat me like this.

G Always up to mischief, aren't you, my poor little darling?

H You really have neglected them.

PAPER 5 SPEAKING

PART 1

Answer these questions about yourself.

Which English-speaking countries have you visited?
Which country do you think you would most like to live in? Why?
How did/would you feel about going abroad and leaving your family and friends behind?
What do/would you like about having a home of your own?

PART 2

Look at the photographs on page 123 and answer one of the following questions. Then answer a different question about the photographs on page 124.

Which job would you prefer? Why?
Which job is the most rewarding/demanding? Why?
Which job deserves the highest status/highest pay? Why?

PART 3

Look at the advertisements and answer the questions which follow them.

URGENTLY NEEDED

Secretary and general assistant
for small family firm.
French an asset.
The successful applicant can
negotiate her pay and
conditions at interview.

Mr Justice: (0120) 54366

SECRETARY WANTED

Each candidate will be
required to demonstrate
his/her knowledge of
French at interview.
Good promotion
prospects for
ambitious employees.

Majesty Holdings: (0154) 30687
(Pay and conditions will be notified at interview.)

Which of the two jobs sounds best? Why do you think so?

PART 4

Answer these questions.

Which is better – work or school?
How could we make work or school more worthwhile?
What are the advantages and disadvantages of being a boss?
What will work be like in the future? What are the dangers of getting computers and robots to do more and more?

For Further Practice and Guidance, see page 116.

FURTHER PRACTICE AND GUIDANCE *(vertical side tab)*

BE A GOOD LISTENER

In Part 4 of Paper 5, the examiner will ask questions that prompt long answers to encourage you and your partner to discuss a topic that is raised in Part 3. Thus Part 3 of the test on page 115 is concerned with jobs and Part 4 asks you to discuss school and employment, status at work and the effects/dangers of modern technology.

Being a good listener is part of your task. If you butt in too much, you may well lose marks. Take in what your partner says and try to find ways to develop his or her ideas. Suppose your partner says:

'I'd hate to be unemployed because I wouldn't know what to do with myself. I'm desperate to get a secure job – something that will keep me going until I eventually retire.'

Here are three possible ways to respond:

a 'Oh, I'm the opposite. To be honest, I'll put off getting a job for as long as I can.'
b 'But when you retire your life will suddenly be very empty.'
c 'The trouble is that these days fewer and fewer jobs are really secure.'

Response **a** is a sort of contradiction; it sounds as if the speaker wants to snatch the topic (or the examiner's attention) from the other person.

Both **b** and **c** might be better. Response **b** could be said in a gentle, enquiring way that would encourage the other speaker to say more. It queries what has just been said but without being too aggressive or contradictory. The other speaker could mention a personal experience and finish by saying: 'Haven't <u>you</u> felt like that?' This is exactly the sort of chance that you and your partner should be giving each other all the time. (If your partner <u>doesn't</u> give you such chances it's your partner, not you, who'll be losing marks. The examiner will see that you do have sufficient chance to speak.)

When looking at pictures, you can often make do with the present tense. A candidate talking about photograph A on page 124 might, for example, say:

'The picture shows a woman, who seems to be teaching a group of girls. In the centre of the picture I can see a TV screen with a map. So she's probably teaching geography, which is a subject I hate.'

Although this sticks to the present tense, it makes a good start to Part 2 of the paper. However, it would probably be hard or impossible to succeed in Parts 3 and 4 without using quite a range of verb forms, including conditionals. This is because you're talking about things you can't see and touch; you haven't even got pictures of them. They're probably in your dreams, in the future or in the past.

Look again at the brief passage beginning 'I'd hate to be unemployed' above and notice the various ways in which it uses verbs. Then, for practice, model a similar statement. Start with 'I'd hate to' or 'I'd love to' and stick quite close to the sentence structures and tenses given – but say what you like!

The photos on this page are for Test One Paper 5 Part 2 on page 30.

The photos on this page are for Test One Paper 5 Part 2 on page 30.

The photos on this page are for Test Two Paper 5 Part 2 on page 60.

The photos on this page are for Test Two Paper 5 Part 2 on page 60.

The photos on this page are for Test Three Paper 5 Part 2 on page 85.

The photos on this page are for Test Three Paper 5 Part 2 on page 85.

The photos on this page are for Test Four Paper 5 Part 2 on page 114.

The photos on this page are for Test Four Paper 5 Part 2 on page 114.

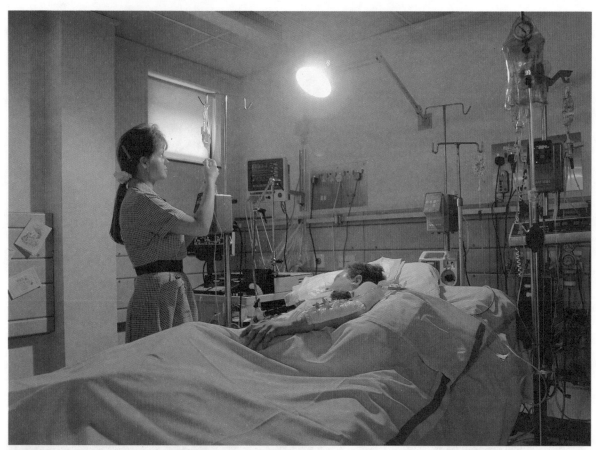

CAMBRIDGE
EXAMINATIONS, CERTIFICATES AND DIPLOMAS
ENGLISH AS A FOREIGN LANGUAGE

**University of Cambridge
Local Examinations Syndicate
International   Examinations**

For Supervisor's use only

Shade here if the candidate is
ABSENT or has WITHDRAWN

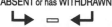

Examination Details	9999/01	99/D99

Examination Title   First Certificate in English

Centre/Candidate No.   AA999/9999

Candidate Name   A.N. EXAMPLE

SAMPLE

• Sign here if the details above are correct

[X]

• Tell the Supervisor now if the details above
  are not correct

Candidate Answer Sheet: FCE Paper 1 Reading

Use a pencil

Mark ONE letter for each
question.

For example, if you think **B** is
the right answer to the
question, mark your answer
sheet like this:

0	A B D

Change your answer like
this:

0	A C D

6	A B C D E F G H I
7	A B C D E F G H I
8	A B C D E F G H I
9	A B C D E F G H I
10	A B C D E F G H I
11	A B C D E F G H I
12	A B C D E F G H I
13	A B C D E F G H I
14	A B C D E F G H I
15	A B C D E F G H I
16	A B C D E F G H I
17	A B C D E F G H I
18	A B C D E F G H I
19	A B C D E F G H I
20	A B C D E F G H I

21	A B C D E F G H I
22	A B C D E F G H I
23	A B C D E F G H I
24	A B C D E F G H I
25	A B C D E F G H I
26	A B C D E F G H I
27	A B C D E F G H I
28	A B C D E F G H I
29	A B C D E F G H I
30	A B C D E F G H I
31	A B C D E F G H I
32	A B C D E F G H I
33	A B C D E F G H I
34	A B C D E F G H I
35	A B C D E F G H I

1	A B C D E F G H I
2	A B C D E F G H I
3	A B C D E F G H I
4	A B C D E F G H I
5	A B C D E F G H I

CAMBRIDGE
EXAMINATIONS, CERTIFICATES AND DIPLOMAS
ENGLISH AS A FOREIGN LANGUAGE

University of Cambridge
Local Examinations Syndicate
International   Examinations

For Supervisor's use only

Shade here if the candidate is
ABSENT or has WITHDRAWN

☒

Examination Details	9999/03	99/D99

Examination Title   First Certificate in English

Centre/Candidate No.   AA999/9999

Candidate Name   A.N. EXAMPLE

SAMPLE

• Sign here if the details above are correct

- -

• Tell the Supervisor now if the details above
  are not correct

Candidate Answer Sheet: FCE Paper 3 Use of English

Use a pencil

For **Part 1**: Mark ONE letter for each question.

For example, if you think **C** is the
right answer to the question,
mark your answer sheet like this:

For **Parts 2, 3, 4** and **5**: Write your
answers in the spaces next to the
numbers like this:

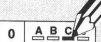

| 0 | A B C |

| 0 | *example* |

Part 1				
1	A	B	C	D
2	A	B	C	D
3	A	B	C	D
4	A	B	C	D
5	A	B	C	D
6	A	B	C	D
7	A	B	C	D
8	A	B	C	D
9	A	B	C	D
10	A	B	C	D
11	A	B	C	D
12	A	B	C	D
13	A	B	C	D
14	A	B	C	D
15	A	B	C	D

Part 2	Do not write here
16	16
17	17
18	18
19	19
20	20
21	21
22	22
23	23
24	24
25	25
26	26
27	27
28	28
29	29
30	30

Turn
over
for
Parts
3 - 5

→

Part 3		Do not write here		
31		31 0	1	2
32		32 0	1	2
33		33 0	1	2
34		34 0	1	2
35		35 0	1	2
36		36 0	1	2
37		37 0	1	2
38		38 0	1	2
39		39 0	1	2
40		40 0	1	2

Part 4	Do not write here
41	41
42	42
43	43
44	44
45	45
46	46
47	47
48	48
49	49
50	50
51	51
52	52
53	53
54	54
55	55

Part 5	Do not write here
56	56
57	57
58	58
59	59
60	60
61	61
62	62
63	63
64	64
65	65

SAMPLE

CAMBRIDGE
EXAMINATIONS, CERTIFICATES AND DIPLOMAS
ENGLISH AS A FOREIGN LANGUAGE

University of Cambridge
Local Examinations Syndicate
International Examinations

For Supervisor's use only

Shade here if the candidate is
ABSENT or has WITHDRAWN

Examination Details	9999/04	99/D99

Examination Title	First Certificate in English

Centre/Candidate No.	AA999/9999

Candidate Name	A.N. EXAMPLE

SAMPLE

• Sign here if the details above are correct

X

- -

• Tell the Supervisor now if the details above
  are not correct

Candidate Answer Sheet: FCE Paper 4 Listening

Mark test version below

A	B	C	D	E

Use a pencil

For **Parts 1** and **3**:
Mark ONE letter for
each question.

For example, if you
think **B** is the right
answer to the
question, mark your
answer sheet like this:

0	A	B	C

For **Parts 2** and **4**:
Write your answers in
the spaces next to the
numbers like this:

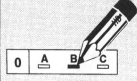

0	example

Part 1

1	A	B	C
2	A	B	C
3	A	B	C
4	A	B	C
5	A	B	C
6	A	B	C
7	A	B	C
8	A	B	C

Part 2 — Do not write here

9		9
10		10
11		11
12		12
13		13
14		14
15		15
16		16
17		17
18		18

Part 3

19	A	B	C	D	E	F
20	A	B	C	D	E	F
21	A	B	C	D	E	F
22	A	B	C	D	E	F
23	A	B	C	D	E	F

Part 4 — Do not write here

24		24
25		25
26		26
27		27
28		28
29		29
30		30

KEY AND EXPLANATION

TEST ONE

P6–7   PAPER 1 PART 1

For Part 1, see also **Further Practice and Guidance** on pages 8–9 and the answers below.

1 G: Note the references to *the 60s and 70s* (line 9) and *now* (line 11).

2 F: The crop is the gardener's reward, and the word *heaped* (line 23) suggests a heavy one.

3 E: The key idea of the paragraph is to squeeze potatoes into the flower border.

4 D: Cousins are relatives, and related plants (eg tomatoes and potatoes) are green cousins.

5 I: *Them* refers to the tubers.

6 A: The second sentence is slightly off the point, but the rest of the paragraph clearly warrants this title.

7 B: Note that clues to answers may be found elsewhere in the text – in this case, the first sentence of the seventh paragraph.

FURTHER PRACTICE AND GUIDANCE

Question 1
1 potatoes are now fashionable
2 sensible people have always eaten potatoes whereas other people are swayed by (dietary) fashion

Question 2
he/she is saying that they are very fine – they are gleaming like gold and the word *specimens* helps to suggest that they are fine examples

Question 3
1 cleverness/resourcefulness
2 squeezing potatoes into the flower border (lines 27–29)
3 shortage of space

Question 4
1 potatoes and tomatoes (line 35)
2 cousins
3 green – it is used to make clear that they are plants

Question 5
they encourage them to sprout

Question 6
1 newer (line 45)
2 buy seed potatoes

Question 7
1 the first sentence of the final paragraph (line 46)
2 A Guide to the Best

P10–11   PAPER 1 PART 2

8 D: We are told that *football was the one thing at which he excelled* (lines 8–9).

A: Halliday's writing is distinctive, not beautiful (line 1).

B: Halliday's behaviour in class can be silly but it doesn't mark him off from the other pupils. Later in the passage it is the others who are behaving badly.

C: Halliday is good at learning poetry by heart but he shows no sign of loving it. His silly behaviour suggests the opposite (line 4).

9 B: According to the passage, *the sports teacher decided that he did not assert himself enough and he made another boy captain* (lines 9–10).

A: There may be signs that Halliday is lazy but the passage does not relate them to the question of being football captain.

C: Jones is bad at other things, but again the passage does not relate them to the question of being football captain.

D: Once more, the thing that matters is relevance.

10 B: Their morale had reached *a fearsome level* (line 16).

A: The girls' success helped to raise the boys' morale but this is not strictly relevant in itself.

C, D: There is no evidence that Kingston, Jones or Halliday felt confident at the start of the match.

11 B: The emphasis is on Jones's goal-scoring (line 17).

A: Jones's team didn't win. The passage states that *Kingston lost* (line 19).

C: See B above. The *good use* (line 17) is in fact the scoring of goals.

D: Though Jones was captain rather than Halliday, this particular match was a triumph for Jones because of his play.

12 C: The key words (spoken by Halliday) are *they're all right now … I've got them lined up* (line 27).

A: They carried on misbehaving after the teacher refused to let them in (line 25).

B: *Superior officer* (line 30) is a joking way of referring to Halliday. Their obedience to Halliday is just a part of their good behaviour. The question asks why they started behaving, and Halliday's words (see C above) provide the explanation.

D: The pupils were cold, but there's nothing to say that this affected the way they behaved.

13 B: The teacher states *the pupil who impressed me most in the end was David Halliday* (line 21), and she goes on to tell the story of Halliday's mastery over the other pupils.

A: The teacher notices it but there's nothing to say she admires it.

C: The teacher may feel that Halliday deserves to be captain but the passage does not show any moment of realization.

D: The teacher seems to think that Halliday deserves a rest after making the others behave but the question refers to art lessons in general. Early in the passage (line 7), it is stated that Halliday spends them reading because he dislikes them – not because he has earned the privilege.

14 A: See 13D above. The words *as usual* (line 31) link Halliday's wish for a nap with his usual aversion to art.

B, C, D: All these things are possible factors but there is no particular evidence for them. (B and D have ideas of deserving after working hard which really reflect the teacher's thinking rather than Halliday's.)

15 D: From first to last the passage is about Halliday, and it culminates in an achievement and a well-deserved rest.

A, B, C: All these possible titles fit particular parts of the passage only.

P12–13 PAPER 1 PART 3

For Part 3, see also **Further Practice and Guidance** on page 14.

16 H: The preceding sentence mentions Henry's childhood and *the rest of his life* (lines 14–15), so something about his adult interest in Robin Hood follows naturally.

17 D: The idea of pouncing on wealthy travellers connects with the idea of *stealing from rich folk* after the gap (lines 21–22).

18 C: The text after the gap defines *porter* (lines 27–28), which is the key idea of C.

19 E: A (*historians*) and E (*they*) both have a suitable noun or pronoun to fit this gap but only E explains why the enthusiasts dislike *this particular episode* (line 33) and contrasts with the sentence after the gap.

20 A: This extract mentions historians and the search for clues, and the passage goes on to give details of this, referring to *they* (the historians) (line 38) after the gap.

21 G: *This* in the extract must refer to a (Robin) Hood who has just been mentioned (line 41). Also, the doubt created in the extract (*We cannot be sure … but it seems very likely*) leads on logically to the words *if so* (line 43) after the gap.

22 I: Though a tempting answer to 21, this extract does not lead on to the words *if so* (line 43). It tends to act more as a 'rounding off' and summary.

FURTHER PRACTICE AND GUIDANCE

See Part 3 above.

P15–16 PAPER 1 PART 4

23, 24, 25 B, D, E (in any order): Note that in C *old-fashioned* (line 36) and *traditional* (line 46) do not equate with *things from the past*.

26 E: With its *unusual plants and birds* (line 77), Sheringham is *an excellent centre for wildlife enthusiasts* (line 78).

27, 28 C, E (in any order): *The Cumbrian coast* provides *a scenic backdrop* (lines 41–43) and *the steep ascent* (line 71) and *wildlife* (line 78) suggest beautiful, unspoilt countryside.

29 C: The *elderly* are specifically mentioned (line 45) and the opening paragraph shows that the town is quiet and relaxing.

30 B: *It is a thriving industrial centre and a busy port* (lines 23–24). (A is a tempting answer, but the Pleasure Beach, though noisy, does not make the town a bustling place with lots going on.)

31 A: This answer is found in B (lines 30–32). Note the need to survey all the evidence in the passage when answering questions.

32 A: The detail given should make it clear that the Pleasure Beach is (much) the same as a fairground (lines 13–15).

33 A: The illuminations are on *in the autumn* (line 12) and the Pleasure Beach is open for *most of the year* (line 13).

34 C: This answer depends on understanding the second half of the final sentence (lines 46–48).

35 B: The style suggests a book rather than a newspaper or leaflet. There are several mentions of history but the concern is with *places which are well worth a visit* (line 5), whatever the reason, so the passage does not come from D, where the history of seaside resorts would be the main focus.

A: Competing resorts would be unlikely to co-operate in publishing such material.

C: There is nothing 'newsy' or topical in the passage. (It could just possibly come from a Sunday supplement, but the writing is a little too colourful and informative for this to be likely.)

D: See A above.

P18 PAPER 2

FURTHER PRACTICE AND GUIDANCE

Assessment of sample answer

1 The letter does most of what the question requires but it does not ask about availability in August. In addition, the enquiry about a discount for the children is not put clearly. The real situation is that the parent wonders whether there would be a discount for sending all three children at once. The letter is rather short, so these two failures show up all the more. There is no credit for adding addresses, which the question says are not required.

2 The letter is arranged and paragraphed in an appropriate way. The first paragraph serves as an introduction to the whole letter, the second describes the children and the third asks for information.

3 The sentence structures are basically correct, though *and* and *but* are overused. There are no linking words like *finally* but they are not really needed. The letter is brief and simple and progresses in a logical way; see, for example, how the second and third sentences of the second paragraph follow on from the first.

4 The vocabulary is adequate.

5 There are several grammatical errors. *The oldest son has been playing football* uses an inappropriate verb form, while *the younger brother keen on fishing* does not use any verb at all. However, *would you tell me the place and what kind of activities they can do and if there is any discount* is good, though it would have been better to have a comma after *place* instead of *and* (see 3 above). Also, the writer does not seem to know that *John* is a boy's name and says that her *daughter* suffers from asthma. Examiners might not penalize this because there are no other clues to the sufferer's sex. However, in the examination as a whole, it is important to pay attention to this kind of detail where it exists (eg his/her pronouns).

6 The style and approach are very appropriate.

P19 PAPER 3 PART 1

1 **B**: Native speakers would say *a house by the sea* but *a field at the top of the cliffs*.

2 **C**: *Time and again* is a set phrase, an idiom.

3 **D**: A *sea breeze* is a gentle wind that blows from the sea in summer. *Wind* and *draught* do not have such pleasant connotations; a *draught* is an unwanted flow of air inside a room.

4 **A**: *Beyond* is used when something is further away than something else that a speaker can see as in the sentence *I could see the chimney not far away and beyond it I could see the river*. *Nearby* would not fit the sentence because it cannot be followed by *us* and *landing among us* might be possible but not *landing in the grass among us*.

5 A: The context shows that the people were moving nearer to the edge of the cliff to throw their plane. Thus the passage is concerned with where the flights began. In any case, the other options would not be very idiomatic or logical.

6 A: C and D cannot be followed by *back*, and B (*took back*) suggests that the wind thinks it owns the plane.

7 B: A (*thought*) does not take *to*. C (*commenced*) implies action which is repeated or takes a while to complete, while D (*tried*) implies an effort which is unsuccessful. The context shows that these two options are inappropriate.

8 B: *Turned out* is idiomatic. The other options combine with *out* but the meanings are inappropriate.

9 D: C (*many*) goes only with nouns. The other options can refer to the repetition of actions but B (*much*) is ruled out here by the presence of *once*. (You can say *you've contradicted me too much* but not *you've contradicted me once too much*.) D is the idiomatic choice in the present context.

10 D: *Made its way* is idiomatic English. The other options do not fit into the context.

11 D: Taking the sentence as a whole, it is clear that the plane has disappeared from sight. The other options do not convey this and A, which suggests only minimal movement, makes little sense with *into the distance*.

12 C: A and D (*now* and *yet*) do not suggest persistence or continuity. B (*staying*) suggests free choice as in *the pilot said he was staying in the air*.

13 C: This suggests random or violent damage. A (*open*) falsely implies that the plane can be opened in some way and D (*up*) would be more suitable for a piece of paper which is being destroyed intentionally.

14 C: *Joy* is a feeling so *feeling* is the obvious choice in this context. D (*sense*) could combine with *joy* in *a sense of joy* but would strike a wrong note in this context.

15 B: *Making a flight* is idiomatic English so C would be the obvious choice. However, the writer of the passage has not made a flight, since he/she has not left the ground. The plane has made the flight and the people have caused it to happen by risking the plane and exploiting the air currents. What happened has been an achievement for them.

P20 PAPER 3 PART 2

For Part 2, see also **Further Practice and Guidance** on page 21.

16 on/during: Both words mean *in the course of* in this context, though *on* has other common meanings too.

17 where: This links the place (*the compartment*) with what was going on there (*six or eight people were sitting*).

18 were: This plural matches the plural *commuters* (see 22 below).

19 except: *Except for* is the standard idiom.

20 hand/hands: Although *dived* is normally used to refer to an aircraft or person plunging downwards, here the verb is used for effect, as the wider context (*into his pockets*) helps to make clear. It is important to read texts both closely and with an overview.

21 Everyone: A tempting alternative answer is *no one*, but again the context makes things clear. (It is important to follow and picture the story, not just to concentrate on grammar and lexis. Remember too to obey the rubric, which here asks for just one word per answer, whereas *no one* is two.)

22 was: The singular form of the verb matches the singular *ticket* (see 18 above).

23 all: *All* can be used with the meaning *all of*.

24 between: Other words like *in*, *inside* or *within* suggest containment. (The ticket could be *inside* the man's mouth but not inside his teeth.)

25 with: This is the usual word to introduce accompanying gestures or actions (*-ing* words like *giving* are tempting but are more appropriate in contexts like *pulling a face, he examined the rotten eggs*).

26 left: This is the obvious word. Some of the possible alternatives (like *gone*) would need to be followed by *from the compartment*.

27 their/the: This is plural because there are several passengers.

28 in/into: Either word is possible here but *into* is better in suggesting movement (compare *it was in his pocket* and *he put it into his pocket*).

29 conversation: *Make conversation* is an established phrase.

30 when/while: *When* is the better answer because it suggests contrast as in *Why did you give me five when I needed six?*.

FURTHER PRACTICE AND GUIDANCE

See Part 2 above.

P22 PAPER 3 PART 3

31 It is **bad for you to eat** too many sweets.

32 He had to **have/get someone to mend** his door.

33 Because of **the/its weight(,) John couldn't/could not** carry the box on his back.

34 The rain **was so heavy (that)** I stayed at home.

35 He **couldn't remember what** Jill's phone number was.

36 Repairing **my roof will cost (me)** a lot of money.

37 I **was woken by the thunder** at seven o'clock.

38 Bloggs **was guilty of (committing)** a serious crime.

39 He had **some flowers in his hand** when he knocked at Margaret's door.

40 The knife **wasn't sharp enough** to cut the bread.

P23 PAPER 3 PART 4

For Part 4 see also **Further Practice and Guidance** on page 24.

41 to: *To stay* would be correct, but the word in the text is *staying* and it needs to be preceded by *of* not *to*.

42 ✓

43 away: The idea of being drawn away is already contained in the word *distract*.

44 ✓

45 ✓

46 will: This is a case where English uses a present tense form for future reference. Another, similar, example would be *even if they want you with them, they won't expect to keep you for nothing*.

47 be: The statement is simply that X can easily lead to Y.

48 you: You can speak of *bad feeling between two people* or you can say *there's a lot of bad feeling in that family* but you can't say something *led them to bad feeling*.

49 be: The passage should read *... can be tricky and embarrassing* (*... can be tricky and can be embarrassing* is possible but awkward).

50 ✓

51 ✓

52 ✓

53 in: You can say *living with* or *living in*, especially in the case of someone (such as an *au pair*) who has work to do at the premises, but *living in with ...* is not normal English.

54 ✓

55 it: *After all* is the standard idiom.

FURTHER PRACTICE AND GUIDANCE

See Part 4 above.

P25 PAPER 3 PART 5

56 relaxation: *Relax/relaxation* and *tax/taxation* are similar pairs. Correct pronunciation will be an aid to memory.

57 unbelievable: This shows the importance of thinking about the sense of the passage and not just making changes mechanically. There may sometimes be cause to add a negative prefix at the start of a word as well as making a change to the end.

58 actually: Adding *-ly* is the commonest way of turning an adjective into an adverb.

59 freshness: Adding *-ness* is a common way of turning an adjective into a noun.

60 explosions: The correct plural form is clear from the following sentence.

61 finally

62 destruction

63 dramatic

64 enjoyable

65 marvellous: The letter *l* is often doubled when an ending is added.

P26–27 PAPER 4 PART 1

The line references are to the tape transcripts on pages 156–157.

1 **C**: The man says *I seem to be allergic to it. It's not the fault of the paint – it's me* (lines 3–4).

2 **C**: The woman mentions *delays* (line 12) (A) and *cancellations* (line 13) (B) but the key factor is that there's *not (an hourly service) on a Sunday* (line 10).

3 **A**: They refer to *the weather* (line 1) (B) and the snowfall in recent years (lines 3–5) (C), but the only thing they argue about is the climate.

4 **A**: The man's references to the law (lines 12–14 and 16–17) suggest that he is a policeman (A) or a judge (C) rather than a garage mechanic (B). The linguistic register and situation – evidently with *this car* on the spot – confirm the answer is A.

5 **B**: The final sentence shows that what's grown is something to eat, and the earlier reference to rubbing the soil off (line 1) suggests that it is some sort of root crop.

6 **A**: Only this would involve the breadth of approach displayed in the passage.

7 **A**: The speaker is drawing metaphors from architecture (B) and gardens (C) but is talking about a piece of music.

8 **B**: The speaker's first idea is A (line 4), but she quickly begins to talk in terms of something having *gone wrong* (line 5). (She can't have a discount but this is not the root of the problem.)

P27 PAPER 4 PART 2

The line references are to the tape transcripts on pages 157–158.

9 **Japan** (line 3)

10 **spare parts** (line 6)

11 **(his firm's/company's) head office (in London)** (lines 7–8)

12 **in/within less than 36 hours** (lines 25–26)

13 **less than £3 a week** (line 50)

14 **paper for the printer (and that sort of thing)** (lines 54–55)

15 **about 300 sheets** (lines 57–58)

16 **£2** (NOT *£2 a roll* because the question includes the words *each roll*) (line 56)

17 **they're/they are (entirely) automatic** (line 62)

18 **knobs and buttons** (lines 63–64)

P28 PAPER 4 PART 3

The line references are to the tape transcripts on pages 158–159.

19 **D**: The speaker refers to *the classic authors* (line 7) and says *I go for books that have been around for quite some time* (lines 4–5). The words *I'm a history fan* (lines 3–4) might suggest F but the speaker doesn't say anything about preferred topics and F appears to refer to non-fiction, while the speaker likes *fiction more than fact* (lines 2–3).

20 **E**: The references to *people* (line 1) and a book *based on fact* (lines 7–8) called *Margery Kempe* (lines 6–7) might suggest C but fiction is clearly the speaker's interest. The words *I'm always on the lookout for a good new novel* (lines 2–3) rule out D.

21 **A**: *A good mystery* (line 1) could refer to fiction but the rest of the statement rules this out.

22 **B**: This is the only answer that explains why the speaker's books, hands and clothes are covered in oil.

23 **C**: The reference to Brunel mentions *technical skill* (line 3) while Margery Kempe is clearly a historical subject. This might suggest B and F respectively, but the common factor is that Brunel and Kempe are both the subject of biographies. See also the speaker's opening and closing remarks.

P28 PAPER 4 PART 4

For Part 4, see also **Further Practice and Guidance** on page 29 and the answers below.

The line references are to the tape transcripts on pages 159–160.

24 **J**: His son asks him why he's *looking so angry* (lines 12–13).

25 **S**: She says *it isn't safe to play in the street* (line 28).

26 J: In particular, he doesn't give Bill a chance to complete his explanation/confession until right at the end.

27 S: She says *I can't help feeling sorry for the lad* (lines 34–35).

28 J: He says *you're being cheeky!* (line 47).

29 B: See 26 above.

30 S: Mrs Smith is the first one to mention *the recreation ground* (lines 54–55).

FURTHER PRACTICE AND GUIDANCE

1 F: Mrs Smith knocks at Mr Jenkins' door.

2 F: Mrs Smith speaks first.

3 T

4 F

5 T: He asks *what's wrong … why are you looking so angry?* (lines 12–13).

6 T

7 F: His father says *it's no good standing there squirming, Bill* (lines 17–18) so it's most unlikely that his face looks innocent (if you squirm, you fidget in a very uncomfortable, embarrassed way).

8 F

9 T

10 F: He mentions her *daffodils* (line 25).

11 T: She says *it isn't just the damage, it's their welfare too. It isn't safe to play in the street* (lines 27–28).

12 T

13 F: Mrs Smith refers to Bill having done so in the past (but see 18 below).

14 T

15 T: Bill says *this time we were kicking the ball up and down the road to avoid it going into the gardens* (lines 38–40).

16 T: What he says (lines 43–46) must be understood in terms of what Mrs Smith has said.

17 T

18 T

19 T

20 T

P32–33 PAPER 5

FURTHER PRACTICE AND GUIDANCE

Start **a** is better. The candidate is making a personal response to the idea of gardening, referring to the picture and then, briefly, to his/her past experience to justify a hatred of what the picture shows. Start **b** uses too many 'locating phrases' like *in the centre*; this goes with a rather bitty description of what is depicted and an absence of any personal response. You should be ready to compare and contrast your responses to the photographs as a pair; you should also be ready to share ideas with your partner when prompted by the examiner.

TEST TWO

P34–35 PAPER 1 PART 1

1 B: A is a tempting answer, but its mention of life goes beyond what the paragraph actually says. Only B really sums the paragraph up for it turns on the contrasts between hot and cold, glare and blackness.

2 A: This time there is a mention of life (line 7).

3 H: The first half of the paragraph presents facts (lines 8–10) and the second presents what could broadly be called fiction (lines 10–12).

4 D: The idea of gases in turmoil is stated in the first two sentences and illustrated in the third.

5 E: Saturn can be *seen and enjoyed with a simple pair of binoculars* (lines 21–22).

6 F: Pluto is both distant and a wanderer.

7 G: The word *unseen* appears in the passage (line 29) and a *mysterious gravitational pull* (line 28) amounts to a definite *influence*.

P36–37 PAPER 1 PART 2

For Part 2, see also **Further Practice and Guidance** on pages 38–39 and the answers below.

8 B: The author wonders when they would find *a real home* (line 24).

A: *Returning in the evening* (line 28) and the presence of children are inconsistent with the place being a prison. See

also B above. The word *inmates* (line 22) does suggest a prison but is clearly used to express the author's feelings.

C: The conditions are far too spartan for this. Again, see B above.

D: The presence of children shows that this is untrue. In any case, there is no sign in the passage of anyone being old.

9 B: See the second paragraph. The warden is using a compressed form of the idiom *has to be seen to be believed*. He's telling the couple they'll have to see how cramped the accommodation is before they believe it. He shakes his head *forlornly* (meaning sorrowfully).

A: In the context, the warden's *Home Sweet Home* (line 9) is clearly ironical.

C: Again, see the second paragraph. At the end of the passage, it seems that the warden has sent some other people to share the accommodation, but that doesn't mean he considers it spacious enough.

D: The warden's last words (lines 11–12) fall well short of praising the furniture.

10 B: *The bedroom was freezing* (line 20) is followed at once by mention of *the top flap of the window* (line 20) being *jammed open by rust* (line 21).

A: The stove is in a different room.

C: With its *meagre blankets* (line 19), the bed would be cold like the rest of the room, but the question applies to the room as a whole.

D: Dust blowing under the front door is going into the front room, so the ill-fitting door may not be affecting the bedroom temperature very much.

11 D: *No two of anything were the same* (lines 13–14).

A, B, C: These may be reasonable guesses but there is no evidence that any of them applies to the furniture in general.

12 A: The author sits on the bed with his head in his hands, wondering how long they would have to spend there (lines 23–24).

B, C, D: There is little sign of optimism, determination (the struggle with the window is very brief) or anger (though there is a half-hearted argument with the new arrivals).

13 B: The cover *looked worse than the stains underneath* (lines 26–27).

A: The blankets were in the cupboard (line 19), not under the plastic cover. The smell of the blankets has nothing to do with removing the cover.

C: After removing the cover from the mattress, the couple add the blankets to the bed to keep themselves warm. Removing the cover has nothing to do with keeping warm.

D: See B above.

14 A: See the tenth paragraph. The couple *peer* (look suspiciously) at *a jumble of people and things and colours* (line 30) and the situation is described as *a muddle* (line 31).

B, C, D: If these occur they come slightly later.

15 C: The final paragraph says so clearly.

A: The bewilderment described in the tenth paragraph suggests that there has been a mistake, but see C above.

B: Taken together, the end of the tenth paragraph and the start of the final paragraph might suggest B, but see C above.

D: A week is up but there is no reason to think that the accommodation is used on a weekly basis.

FURTHER PRACTICE AND GUIDANCE

Question 8

1 A warder supervises prisoners in a jail, but the passage uses *warden* (line 1) instead so A (*a prison*) is probably incorrect.

2 *I hope you can make a go of it* (line 11) means *I hope you can manage* which contradicts C and possibly A and D.

3 The author has used inverted commas to show that he doesn't mean *cell* (lines 13 and 17) in its literal sense but just for effect. The word *inmate* (line 22) is used in a similar way.

Question 9
Most of what the warden says contradicts the idea that this is cosy accommodation. When he says *Home Sweet Home* (line 9) he is being ironical, in other words saying the opposite of what he means for effect.

Question 10
B and C relate to the bedroom, A and D relate to other parts of the accommodation.

Question 11

1 D – the first thing the author notices about the furniture is that *no two of anything were the same* (lines 13–14).

2 The reference to *furniture from a charity shop* (line 14) follows the author's first comment after nothing more than a semi-colon, so the whole sentence supports D. The author's main impression is that nothing matches anything else.

Question 12
A. The answer is not stated directly but the man's feelings are implied by his actions.

Question 13

1 The text implies that after removing the plastic cover the couple make the bed.

2 Spreading the blankets releases their smell.

Question 14

1 The people are first described as *a jumble* (line 30) (mixed up with other things and colours) and the word *muddle* (line 31) is used soon afterwards, supporting A.

2 The words *jumble* (line 30) and *muddle* (line 31) link with the word *confusion* in A.

Question 15
The word is *accommodation* (line 37), which could be added after *share* (line 35).

P40 PAPER 1 PART 3

16 B: *Mere seasonal changes* (line 5) is a reference back to the mention of variation in B.

17 C: Before the gap the passage mentions shallow wells and after the gap it says that deeper ones have taken their place.

18 E: The mention of a drop of 20 metres in E logically follows the mentions of water at depths of five metres (line 9) and 25 metres (line 11).

19 D: This extract continues the description of *a vicious circle* (line 12).

20 F: The passage goes on after the gap with *nowadays, though* (line 16) and is clearly contrasting present unproductiveness with something better in the past.

21 A: *So, too* in A means that it must follow something similar to what has gone before. The passage before the gap mentions a fall in the amount of wildlife (lines 17–18) and A mentions a corresponding fall in the human population.

P43–44 PAPER 1 PART 4

For Part 4, see also **Further Practice and Guidance** on page 45 and the answers below.

22, 23 C, D (in any order): Brought indoors in autumn, busy lizzies *will carry on flowering indefinitely* (line 34) and potentillas *stay in bloom almost ceaselessly* (lines 48–49).

24 C: See the first paragraph (line 3).

25 C: See 22 above.

26 B: *The short-lived flowers make a real midsummer spectacle* (lines 25–26).

27, 28, 29 C, D, E (in any order): See the last two sentences of C and D (lines 39 and 51) and the height measurement given in E (line 58).

30, 31 C, E (in any order): See the latter half of C (lines 36–37) for both these answers.

32 A: The word *stored* goes with saving inert tubers (line 12), rather than keeping plants alive and more or less active.

33, 34 A, C (in any order): The passage says that the tubers (line 12) or plants (line 32) need bringing indoors.

35 D: This is the only plant where the seed is sown the previous year (line 44).

FURTHER PRACTICE AND GUIDANCE

Questions 36 and 37
A (the flowers are *showy)* (line 6) and B (*the spikes of colour* are *fine* and *dazzling* and *make a real midsummer spectacle*) (lines 20–26)

P47 PAPER 2

FURTHER PRACTICE AND GUIDANCE

Assessment of sample answer

1 The answer does almost everything the question asks, though the point about nearness to the college is missed.

2 The answer is not in paragraphs. The arrangement – starting with a reference to the advertisement and a self-introduction, and moving on to a long string of questions – is just acceptable. However, the questions could have been grouped – and paragraphed – by theme.

3 The sentence structures are simple and basic, and questions and remarks are fired in a rather quick-shot way. However, there is some linkage between sentences (*another thing I wish to ask you is ..., also I want to ask you ..., and finally I want to ask you ...*).

4 The vocabulary is correctly used but it is not very adventurous.

5 There are some serious mistakes with prepositions. At the start of the letter, *I'm writing to ask you for your advertisement* should be *I'm writing to ask you about your advertisement* and, a little later, *I will stay in England very long time* omits the words *for a*.

6 The style is not appropriate. It would probably be better to start a business letter to a stranger with the more formal *I am* rather than *I'm. O.K.*, like *I'm*, is too informal, and *O.K. let's go to details* is rather brisk. (It makes a link but a break of paragraph would have been better). Also the expression *to go into detail* is not appropriate in this context. *I want to ask you when I can come* is again too informal; it would be better to say *I would like to ask you when I could come.*

P48 PAPER 3 PART 1

For Part 1, see also **Further Practice and Guidance** on page 49.

1 B: *Cause for complaint* is almost a set phrase whereas *reason for* would be followed by *complaining*. (We *make* or *raise an objection*, but this applies to a plan or procedure and rarely to goods and services.)

2 B: *Of* always follows *way* and other such words before *-ing*.

3 A: C and D would be grammatical but rather too formal. Also, *conversation* suggests a thorough or wide-ranging discussion. A is better because it implies that what's said is brief and specific.

4 C: *There's every chance* is idiomatic. (D could be used in a slightly different context with *I* as in *I've every intention of ...*)

5 D: The other options would follow other verbs. A (*need*) could be used after *meet*, B (*breakdown*) could be used after *repair* and C (*fault*) could be used after *rectify*.

6 C: A and B are so vague as to sound odd. D could be used in the context *if goods arrive broken* (though *damaged* would be a more likely word).

7 D: Only this word builds on what has gone before.

8 A: *Collect* is a suitable word because it sees things as much from the customer's point of view as the company's. C and D over-emphasize the company's viewpoint and imply that they have an urgent need to lay their hands on the goods in question. B is too vague (though *take away* would have been acceptable).

9 **C**: A and B over-emphasize attendance at a certain place and the point is simply that the MD is willing to meet whoever wants to see him. D (*seen*) could be used after *may be* but not after *is*.

10 **A**: The others cannot (with appropriate meaning) be followed by *with*.

11 **C**: A (*respect*) could be used in the context *in which respect are you dissatisfied with our service?* but not in this context.

12 **B**: A (*writing*) is followed by *to* and C (*speaking*) is followed by *to* or *with*. D (*consulting*) implies a balanced exchange but the passage speaks of *letting us know*, which is more one-sided.

13 **D**: This is the only grammatical option out of those offered to convey the sense of making better.

14 **B**: A (*used*) and C (*employed*) do not convey the sense of acceptance at the meeting itself. D (*allowed*) is usually followed by *to* and a verb.

15 **A**: *This* is idiomatic, B (*idea*) would give the clause a different meaning; the other answers would hardly make sense.

FURTHER PRACTICE AND GUIDANCE

See Part 1 above.

P50 PAPER 3 PART 2

16 **imagine**: *Think* may perhaps be possible but is poorer, less lively.

17 **as**: NOT *for*.

18 **it**: *When it comes to* is an idiomatic expression.

19 **another**: This is another example of the need to consider this longish sentence as a whole.

20 **the**: *All the rage* is an idiomatic expression.

21 **spite**: Again this is a set phrase.

22 **never/don't**: *Hardly* is grammatical but there's nothing to suggest that there's ever any change whatever.

23 **than**

24 **treat**: Compare *treat it with caution* and *handle it with care*.

25 **with**

26 **in**: This part of the passage is not easy and it helps to picture the overall context.

27 **if**: Answers like *because* are wrong as they imply that the car is sure to be one of the *danger colours*, whereas the passage envisages various possibilities.

28 **when/though/if**

29 **hardly**: Compare *hardly ever* and *almost never*.

30 **so**: With the sense *so much*.

P51 PAPER 3 PART 3

For Part 3, see also **Further Practice and Guidance** on page 52.

31 It **was necessary for the firemen** to break the door down. (The correct pattern is *necessary for someone to do something*.)

32 It's **the first time I've ever** eaten walnuts. (*Ever* in positive statements contrasts with *never* in negative statements.)

33 There's **no doubt (that) Tom was** first in the queue. (*Doubt* can be qualified in all sorts of ways – *there's a lot of/some/little/no doubt* would all be grammatical. The word *definitely* in the cue sentence requires *no* in this instance.)

34 Mary **has a lot of/many acquaintances** in France. (You *know* people but you *have* acquaintances.)

35 Anthony **made a journey/ went on a journey** to Spain. (Both options are idiomatic.)

36 The books were **too expensive for me** to buy. (*Too* with an adjective is often followed by *for* as in *too cold for swimming* or the idiomatic *too unpleasant for words*.)

37 I couldn't **put up with** the noise any longer. (*Put up with* is a set expression.)

38 I told John **to come to me** with his problems. (*Bring* can often be changed to *come with* as in *I wonder when the delivery men will bring/come with my furniture*.)

39 I **reduced my speed** at the traffic lights. (*Reduce* and *increase* are the usual words to use when referring to changes of *speed*.)

40 I couldn't **make sense of** what I was reading. (*That doesn't make sense* and *it makes sense to me* are idiomatic. (*Of* in this answer means *out of* or *from*. *Of* is frequently used when we talk about changing the state of something, as in *don't make a mess of your homework*.)

FURTHER PRACTICE AND GUIDANCE

See Part 3 above.

P54 PAPER 3 PART 4

41 ✓

42 of: It is correct to say *we make use of them* or *we use them* but not *we use of them*.

43 to: The second *to* is inessential as the first can do service for both positions. However, the structure is clearer with both included.

44 up: *Come up to* is appropriate if we are talking about approaching a person for some sort of encounter. *Don't cross your bridges before you come to them* is a well-known figure of speech. Its use of *come to them* is perfectly regular.

45 much: *Doing so* means *doing it*.

46 ✓

47 above: *Over* and *above* mean much the same so only one is required at this point. *Over* would be the more regular choice though *above* is possible.

48 ✓

49 the: *Information, advice …* are not an established topic in the passage, whereas *the* implies that they are.

50 ✓

51 been: You can say *he would have been used to this book (for years)* but the word *to* does not appear in the passage and the meaning is different.

52 more: *Improve* already carries the sense of *more* and *improve more* could only be used if you were talking about a further improvement on top of one already made.

53 ✓

54 to: *Put you in touch* is the normal form.

55 at: *At present* means *now* or *currently*. Here the passage is referring to the present (time). The word *the* could have been used before *present* but *the* before *past* is understood to apply here too.

P55 PAPER 3 PART 5

56 failure

57 perseverance

58 behaviour

59 simplicity

60 patience

61 annoyance

62 foolishly: Compare *-ally* at the end of 65.

63 marvellous

64 invention

65 personally: Compare *-ly* at the end of 62.

P56–57 PAPER 4 PART 1

The line references are to the tape transcripts on pages 160–162.

1 B: He says that on his return his *machine should be free of all its gremlins* – even if he's *still under the weather* (lines 24–26).

2 A: He begins by saying *let's put it this way, some people can and some people can't* (lines 1–2). The context, right through to the final word *nightcap*, shows that he is referring to sleep. (*Let's put it this way* shows that the subject was established even before the extract opened.) The effects of tea and coffee are clearly cited just to expand this theme.

3 B: He says he finds it *hard to remember* (line 6) when he last saw her. A is totally wrong. He *never noticed the state of her hair* (lines 16–17) so he can't be claiming to have forgotten it.

4 C: At the end of the extract she's obviously dismayed. Note her stumbling speech and her use of the obvious, weak word *nice* (line 18). It's the best she can manage when she feels so 'let down'.

5 A: The lecturer tells the students to *divide yourselves up into twos and threes and some study one topic while others study another one* (lines 16–18). That way, they can borrow the books they need from the library *in turn* (line 19).

6 C: The golfer confesses *it could be the fact that I've lost a lens from my glasses* (lines 13–14) and his companion clearly thinks the same!

7 C: According to Mr Fergusson, it's up to the wise purchaser to *consider the state of the market* (line 24) at the time he buys.

8 A: The news report says that the action was *a protest over rising water bills* (lines 9–10). The matter of waste is touched on but is less important. It could be a cause of rising bills but the point isn't raised by the protestor himself.

P57 PAPER 4 PART 2

The line references are to the tape transcripts on pages 163–165.

9 she has (just) phoned (line 1)

10 (just over) two hours (this is the gap between the times mentioned in lines 3 and 6)

11 watched sport (on television) (lines 11–12)

12 the poor (quality of the) food (lines 15–16)

13 the cost/the fact that he (probably) can't afford it (lines 16–17)

14 the 'local' television studios (lines 19–20)

15 the Science Museum (line 29)

16 shape(s) and sizes(s) (line 35)

17 closes at five o'clock/will be closed (lines 43–44)

18 (professional) musicians (lines 48–49)

P58 PAPER 4 PART 3

The line references are to the tape transcripts on page 164.

19 B: The fire brigade isn't mentioned by name but is indicated by the words *klaxons* (line 12) (sirens) and *appliance* (line 13) and also by its role of rescuer. (On a literal interpretation, the rescuers are *the crowds of children* (line 14), but excited oral delivery brings looseness of grammar and a good listener makes allowance for this.)

20 A: The key words are *so that's why I'm looking for another job* (lines 11–12). The speaker uses some difficult phrases but the gist of the passage (and reading for gist is an important skill to cultivate) should still be clear. (Note the word *sack* in A is not associated with Speaker 4, who wears a sack while his clothes are drying. *The sack* is a common term for dismissal.)

21 D: The words *just when I thought I'd managed to dodge the thunderstorm I was drenched* (lines 4–6) might suggest C but it is, of course, important to take the passage as a whole, including its reference to *the tin* (line 3) and the *red … sticky mess* (lines 11–12). Its being *a sort of fashion shade* (line 11) is an added clue.

22 C: The references to *a deluge* (line 1), *tumble drying* (lines 14–16) and being *under cover at last* (line 17) are important indicators. The statement *it was just as though I'd taken a fully clothed dip in the lake* (lines 3–4) helps to rule out F since *just as though* indicates that this is not what actually happened. However, careless listeners may gain the wrong impression here.

23 E: *The (fluorescent) red was over everywhere* (lines 6–7).

P58 PAPER 4 PART 4

The line references are to the tape transcripts on page 165.

24 P: She thinks Mrs Turnbull is in favour of the road (line 8).

25 I: He calls the passer-by Mrs Turnbull (line 25).

26 T: She represents BATT (Bradley Action for Tunnel Transport) (line 40).

27 T: She mentions *several rare species of wild flower* (line 60).

28 T: She says that under the proposal the existing main road would only be moved *by a few hundred yards* (line 50).

29 I: He says *the road could be raised over any sites of special interest* (lines 63–64).

30 P: The inspector seems more interested in listening to Mrs Turnbull (lines 76–77).

FURTHER PRACTICE AND GUIDANCE

1 Speakers 1, 3 and 5

2 Speaker 1

3 Speaker 1: Among other things she creates suspense. This begins with her very first sentence *and then it happened* (line 1), which makes the hearer inquisitive.

4 Speaker 2: He says *of course,*

I can't complain ... it's my fault I hadn't read the instructions ... I was really the cause of it all (lines 1, 2–3 and 8) and he describes being sacked as *harsh but not completely unfair* (lines 10–11).

5 Speaker 3

6 Speaker 4: There are touches of humour from other speakers but Speaker 4 has most as in *it was just as good as some of the latest fashions from Paris ... I sat there like a load of potatoes ... I could have done with a bit of tumble drying myself* (lines 7–8, 13–14 and 15–16).

P62 PAPER 5

FURTHER PRACTICE AND GUIDANCE

1 I'm 20 years old and I've been living in London since last year.

2 I'm studying English at Lexicon College.

3 I live at home on the opposite side of the city.

4 I don't have a car so I get to the college on foot or by bus.

5 If I pass my exams I'll be able to take a secretarial course.

TEST THREE

P63–64 PAPER 1 PART 1

For Part 1, see also **Further Practice and Guidance** on page 65 and the answers below.

1 G: *Putting friends to the test* is a negative thing. You're putting them to trouble and they may not be your friends for much longer! See the final sentence (lines 5–7).

2 C: See the final sentence (lines 12–15).

3 D: The *10, 15 or 30 minutes* (lines 20–21) suggests how the waiting goes on and on, and the repeated word in D has the same effect.

4 E: Again, see the final sentence (lines 31–32). (A final sentence can often sum up a paragraph and suggest an appropriate heading.)

5 B: The word *fume* is sometimes used to refer to a state when a person can hardly control his anger. He doesn't explode but he's obviously angry! Here it can have that meaning but can also refer to exhaust fumes, so the heading is a sort of pun.

6 A: The *word* is *about* (line 44).

7 F: The passage could have continued *so it's up to you to be there on time*.

FURTHER PRACTICE AND GUIDANCE

1 fourth paragraph, after *letting him down* (line 32)

2 first paragraph, before the third sentence (line 3)

3 second paragraph, at the end (line 15)

4 third paragraph, after *wasted time* (line 26)

5 fifth paragraph, at the end (line 39)

6 seventh paragraph, at the end (line 59)

7 sixth paragraph, at the beginning of the final sentence (line 47)

P66–67 PAPER 1 PART 2

8 B: The first paragraph links his depression with the problem of keeping a steady job and, in the words of the fifth paragraph, *the fear of being 'out' haunted him all the time* (line 16).

A: It had been a bad summer because of the constant need to find new work. If Easton now had a permanent job, he would not be depressed, but in fact he is *haunted* by the *fear of being 'out'* (line 16).

C: The statement is true but is not in itself a cause of depression. Having a wife just increases his fear of unemployment.

D: There is nothing to say that the pain of walking had made him depressed.

9 A: The paragraph speaks of being *out of work* (line 14) then abbreviates it to *'out'* (line 16).

B, C, D: The passage does not support these answers, even though they may suggest idioms like *out of money* and *falling out*. *Out of work* (line 14) is the only *out*

(line 16) idiom which is used and then abbreviated in the passage.

10 B: From the seventh paragraph it is clear that Hunter was Crass's superior.

A: Jack Linden had been dismissed, presumably by Crass, so he must have been less senior than Crass and Hunter.

C: See B above.

D: Easton could be dismissed at Crass's instigation, just as Linden had been, so he, too, must have been less senior than Crass and Hunter.

11 C: See the seventh paragraph. *Tones, shades* and *harmony* (lines 27–28) are terms connected with colour schemes.

A: It was by using language cleverly that Crass won Hunter's favour, but Hunter was probably not aware of this or he wouldn't have been taken in.

B: Crass had skills as a manager but the passage doesn't say that Hunter was aware of these.

D: Through laziness, Crass didn't even show what practical skills he had. There is no evidence that Hunter credited him with any.

12 C: *He (Easton) would have to be very careful not to offend Bill Crass in any way* (lines 21–22). It is implied that Jack Linden had already lost his job through offending Crass.

A: Crass got people sacked on the grounds that they were *no good* (line 32) or *too slow for a funeral* (lines 32–33), but they could be accused of this even if they did work hard. (One imagines that Crass's pals could get away with laziness.)

B: Some men managed to stay in Crass's favour *by giving him pipefuls of tobacco and pints of beer* (line 35) but the question asks about *anyone working under Crass*.

D: It was Crass who tried to make room for his pals and this was done by sacking the existing workers.

13 C: *Crass ... was quite without special abilities* (line 25) and he *did as little as possible* (line 31).

A, B, D: See C above.

14 B: The final half sentence (lines 37–38) sums up the passage and ties in with its opening words.

A: Crass is the cause of Easton's uncertain future but the uncertain future is what matters most.

C: These insulting words are just a detail of Crass's techniques and they probably aren't even true of anyone.

D: This is a tempting answer, but the passage gives little external detail of the walk. Instead, it is taken up with Easton's thoughts about his uncertain future and the reasons for it.

P68 PAPER 1 PART 3

For Part 3, see also **Further Practice and Guidance** on page 69.

15 F: It makes the link between life being easier and the problem of his head colliding with light bulbs.

16 D: The link is in the idea of injuries.

17 E: The injuries are explained at last (and the word *trimmed* introduces the use of blades).

18 B: The first half of this paragraph goes into detail about how Uncle Bill used to cut himself.

19 G: This fits in with the ideas of haste and clumsiness which occur both before and after the gap.

20 C: The passage goes on to expand on the idea in C that Uncle Bill's visits to hospital weren't connected with his heart condition.

21 A: This completes the writer's conclusions about his uncle's heart.

FURTHER PRACTICE AND GUIDANCE

See Part 3 above.

P70–71 PAPER 1 PART 4

22, 23 A, E (in any order): Both paragraphs use the word *traditional* (lines 2 and 72) and in this case the obvious answers are right, though sensitive reading is always needed to guard against traps.

24, 25 B, E (in any order): Sandra's prices are *down-to-earth* (line 21) and Margery *charges so little* (lines 82–83).

26 E: The passage says that muffins are among the *range of traditional cakes* offered at Margery's Tea Room (lines 72–73).

27 A: *The tarmac outside fills with modern cars* (lines 12–13).

28 B: Near the end of the paragraph we're told that cigarette smoke *often fills the air* (line 29).

29 C: The evidence is near the end of D (lines 64–66).

30 C: The words *sumptuous* (line 45), *plush* (line 45) and *velvetized* (line 46) are difficult words, but the fact that the carpets and wallpaper are being featured should give a clue, as should the broader context of *exemplary* facilities (line 34) and *superb cuisine* (line 50).

31 D: The paragraph mentions the *needlessly brisk service* (line 63).

32, 33 C, D (in any order): The Bon Hommie has *a chef who consults you* (line 35) and Hambre has a *genuine interest in his customers' reactions* (line 60).

34 E: D is a tempting answer, but only E conveys the homeliness implied by the term *home-made*. Margery is the only *resident chef and proprietor* (lines 76–77).

35 D: Hambre is an *artist by training and still a painter in his spare time* (lines 67–68).

P73 PAPER 2

FURTHER PRACTICE AND GUIDANCE

Assessment of sample answer

1 The student obviously knows what is wanted and has given a very competent answer. There is nothing irrelevant and almost nothing has been misunderstood or omitted. (The question *when start?*, noted on the advertisement, refers to the starting date of the job but the writer asks only about the hours when he should help with the children, so there seems to be some slight misunderstanding or omission here.)

2 The paragraphing is fairly good. In the first two paragraphs the student states his reason for writing and introduces himself. (He mentions his studies and language abilities in both paragraphs and this material could have been better organized.) In the third paragraph he describes some relevant experience and in the fourth he asks some relevant questions.

3 The sentence structures are mostly correct and are quite varied, though *I would like to ask/am asking about ... what kind of* makes the final paragraph awkward and disconnected, despite its satisfactory use of *moreover* and *lastly*.

4 There is a good range of vocabulary and apart from *boy* (first paragraph) and *how* (at the end of the fourth paragraph) it is used correctly.

5 Apart from the defect mentioned in 3, the grammar is mainly correct.

6 The style is appropriately semi-formal, including *I would like to ask* in the fourth paragraph as well as the incorrect *I am asking about*.

P74 PAPER 3 PART 1

1 **B**: C does not convey the idea of a sustained *lying in wait*, while A and D suggest too intense a scrutiny.

2 **C**: This suggests the boy's impatience.

3 **D**: A cannot be followed by an indication (like *on the doormat*) of where the post landed.

4 **A**: C would normally be followed by an object except in a context like '*What have you got in your hand?*' '*Come and see.*'

5 **B**: This is idiomatic usage.

6 **A**: This is idiomatic, and none of the other options can be followed by *me*.

7 **B**: This is the only option which fits the *as ... to as possible* context.

8 **C**: *As possible* is a concise, almost compressed idiom. A could be used in the context *as I was able*, and B and D could be used in the context *as I (possibly) could*.

9 **D**: *Treated with respect* is idiomatic. A suggests how a person or delicate thing should be handled, B suggests a physical danger and C suggests regard for a highly respected person.

10 **D**: It's idiomatic to speak of there being (or not being) *harm in* something.

11 **D**: This is the only option that suggests both the severing and the taking away. (A would suggest the taking away; B and C would suggest the severing if they were followed by *off*.)

12 **C**: This is idiomatic usage. (The other options are more or less grammatical and might be correctly understood, though B suggests an effort to retain a memory against the odds as in *holding the telephone number in my mind was difficult because of the loud music.*)

13 **A**: *Asked* would also have been acceptable, but though C and D mean the same as *asked* in some contexts they will not do here. B means *told* and the context raises the question of asking the parents' permission, not just telling them.

14 **C**: A is only grammatical in the context *after lunch/dinner* etc. B is unacceptable stylistically. D is grammatical but there is nothing to indicate that the event was particularly soon.

15 **B**: This word implies dawning consciousness, which would have to come before anything else. The other things might follow, but there is no evidence that they did.

P75 PAPER 3 PART 2

For Part 2, see also **Further Practice and Guidance** on page 76.

16 possible: See 8 above.

17 ability/power

18 simply/just/merely: Answers like *easily* are wrong because of the comma.

19 glass

20 spate/number/lot

21 full

22 Look/Watch

23 above

24 find: *You shouldn't find it too expensive* or *you shouldn't find the exam too hard* show *find* being used with a subtler sense than the usual one of rediscovering something that's lost. It refers to finding something out.

25 will

26 rest/remainder: *Rest* is the more obvious and idiomatic.

27 because

28 does

29 mean

30 wonder: *No wonder* followed by a verb phrase is a common idiomatic exclamation.

FURTHER PRACTICE AND GUIDANCE

See Part 2 above.

P77 PAPER 3 PART 3

31 You should **speak to her** on the telephone.

32 John **and I live close to** each other.

33 I **told her where** I lived.

34 There's **something wrong with your** brakes.

35 He took two hours **to make/making up his mind** which seeds to buy.

36 It cost me £200 **to have my house repaired** after the storm.

37 The **number of people in Spain** is increasing.

38 It **is/'s time (that)** the train arrived.

39 You should **become a member of** the football club.

40 I **didn't think I'd/I would** win.

P78 PAPER 3 PART 4

41 ✓

42 ✓

43 has: *Have become* from the previous line is understood at this point.

44 of: You say *there are thousands/millions of cars* but *there are two million cars*.

45 ✓

46 ✓

47 the: The packets involved are not particular ones, so *the* is wrong.

48 up: *Up in the air* is just possible, but not *up the air*.

49 a: *In fact* is a standard idiom.

50 ✓

51 hard: If *hard* was correctly used in this line it would come after *working*.

52 bad: *Less badly polluting* is possible, but pollution is bad by definition so no adverb is needed.

53 forward: The meaning of this is already contained in the word *advance*.

54 ✓

55 of: *Of* is not used after *few* or *little* if a noun follows immediately. Thus it is correct to say *a few potatoes*, *a little cheese*, *a few of them* and *a little of the sauce* but not *very little of pollution*.

P79 PAPER 3 PART 5

For Part 5, see also **Further Practice and Guidance** on page 80 and the answers below.

56 confidence

57 easier

58 preparation

59 preferably

60 security

61 unnatural

62 attention

63 beginner: Note the *-nn-* in *beginner* and *beginning*.

64 nervousness

65 comedian

FURTHER PRACTICE AND GUIDANCE

66 persistence

67 steadier

68 compensation

69 reservable

70 purity

71 natural

72 invention

73 winner

74 cheerfulness

75 musician

P81–82 PAPER 4 PART 1

The line references are to the tape transcripts on pages 166–167.

1 **C**

2 **C**: *You'll arrange with another firm yourself?* (line 7) is the key sentence.

3 **A**: *This time they're just too badly decayed to preserve any longer* (lines 6–8).

4 **B**: Peter's success in French will *please Dad most* but the question asks about *the most surprising improvement in Peter's work.*

5 **A**: The instructor says *concentrate on building up the pace and the rhythm* (lines 12–13) and the next two speeches (lines 14–15 and 16) confirm the answer is A.

6 **C**: See the man's longest speech (lines 7–12). B is tempting if *gone from my own pocket* (lines 11–12) is taken too literally and A is

tempting if the first speech is taken out of context.

7 **B**: Having worked out the flight plan (which involves changing at Dresden for Moscow), the travel agent ends by mentioning the time for reaching Amsterdam Airport, which is the starting point not the destination.

8 **C**: See the final sentence.

P82 PAPER 4 PART 2

The line references are to the tape transcripts on pages 167–168.

9 **spend unwisely/spend too much on one or two items** (lines 1–9)

10 **car boot sales/flea markets/ jumble sales** (lines 10–11)

11 **car boot sales/flea markets/ jumble sales** (lines 10–11)

12 **a fiver/five pounds/£5 on you/him** (line 15)

13 **judging character** (line 20)

14 **disappoint you** (lines 27–28)

15 **squander the proceeds/ spend what you get for them** (lines 34–36)

16 **go for quantity/buy lots of cheap things** (lines 40–41)

17 **grandfather clocks** (lines 49–50)

18 **insurance policy** (line 52)

P83 PAPER 4 PART 3

The line references are to the tape transcripts on pages 168–169.

19 C: The mention of *glue* (line 4) is an important clue. The fact that ships are involved might suggest F but these are model ships not actual sailing ships.

20 A: *Dying* (line 1), *go brown round the edges* (line 2), and *lack of water* (line 3) indicate this answer.

21 E: This is eventually confirmed by the words *striding* (line 14) and *hobbling* (line 14).

22 D: This is clear from the mention of *gears* (line 7), *the pedal power to manage most gradients* (lines 8–9) and getting off *for a rest* (line 10). A is tempting because of the horticultural references, but the question asks about hobbies not business activities and the horticulture is clearly the latter.

23 B: *Flat out* (line 6), *fast trot* (line 6) and the idea of building up speed over the years (lines 10–11) should make this clear. (You would not be expected to know the word *pedometer* (line 4) but the passage gives an indication of what it means.)

P83 PAPER 4 PART 4

The line references are to the tape transcripts on pages 169–170.

24 A: She isn't satisfied with Jenny's first offer of £5 (lines 13–14).

25 A: She talks about recommending Quickfire Taxis to Jenny (among others) (lines 23–25) though in fact Jenny didn't need the recommendation.

26 J: She holds it so that Kenneth, the taxi driver, can get through with the chair (line 28).

27 J: She says she was talking with him while waiting for Kenneth to pick her up (line 31).

28 T: He says *if you want people to be friendly to you, you have to be prepared to do things for them* (lines 34–36).

29 T: He comments on an old lady's spending both to her and to Ann and Jenny (lines 45–47).

30 J: She says *I need a few home comforts after all this shopping. It's time to put my feet up and have a jolly good rest* (lines 54–57).

FURTHER PRACTICE AND GUIDANCE

1 a 6, b 5, c 4, d 2, e 3, f 1

2 Less feeling comes over in the remaining two situations because the speakers are giving facts and ideas which aren't particularly personal.

3 **1 I**: The customer's point is that she doesn't want the trouble of coming back to the shop *again*.

2 B: The man is praising the service he is getting.

3 D: *Down in the mouth* means *unhappy*. This time the expression is especially appropriate because the patient is unhappy about the prospect of having dental treatment.

4 C: Peter has finally succeeded with his school work.

5 G: The instructor uses precisely these words.

6 F: The man is afraid he will have to pay out of his wages if a customer succeeds in cheating.

7 H: The travel agent is helping the customer to save time by choosing the right flights.

8 A: *Food for thought* is an expression meaning *something to make you think hard*. In this case there is a play on words because the passage ends on the subject of food.

P87 PAPER 5

FURTHER PRACTICE AND GUIDANCE

1 Playing with his football boots, the boy breaks a lace and loses a stud.

2 He can't attend to his lesson because he's thinking of football.

3 At the end of the lesson his teacher delays him and

4 by the time he reaches the changing room his boots have gone.

5 He goes out onto the football field and shows the teacher the irregular imprint made by his boot (which is being worn by another pupil).

The stud-marks show that the boots are now on the wrong pair of feet! Another clue is the fancy bag seen in pictures 1 and 4. It seems that its string has been used to replace the broken lace, so the culprit is probably the owner of the bag (and his face is seen in picture 1).

TEST FOUR

P 88–89 PAPER 1 PART 1

1 **A**: From the understated first sentence (*organizing a holiday isn't the easiest task in the world*) (lines 1–2) to the uncompromising last (*planning a holiday can be a real pain*) (line 10), the passage clearly refers to the trouble involved in organizing holidays, and it ends by referring to the resultant reward. (Note that the word *price* in A has a very broad meaning and can do so in other contexts too.)

2 **C**: The final sentence seems to be more general than just a reference to health; *disaster* in the passage (line 18) and *the worst* in C are closely matched in their meaning and vagueness. (B is a poorer answer because the passage has nothing to do with prevention. It is true that doctors effect cures, but taken as a whole the phrase *prevention is better than cure* is inappropriate, especially as it is a figure of speech referring to problem-solving in general.)

3 **D**: The person *stuck in a lay-by many miles from home* (lines 20–21) is stranded.

4 **F**: A straightforward answer as long as the words *no vacancy* (line 31) are understood. These are the words displayed at boarding houses and inns when all the accommodation has been taken.

5 **E**: The *bull* (line 39) is the unwelcome visitor. (G is also a tempting answer, but the passage does not refer to

forgetting to book but to deciding *we can't be bothered* to book) (lines 41–42).

6 **H**: This heading is a figurative way of summing up the situation of having no food (line 52).

7 **G**: Unlike the fifth paragraph, this clearly does refer to the various heavy costs of forgetting to do things and forgetting to bring things.

P90–91 PAPER 1 PART 2

For Part 2, see also **Further Practice and Guidance** on pages 92–93 and the answers below.

8 **B**: Churchill says *I have thought it right to bring the whole together in a single complete story* (lines 4–5).

A: The story is of Churchill's early life (only) and does not contain many *modern pronouncements* (line 12).

C: He says he has verified his facts (line 6) but this is not represented as the reason for writing the new account.

D: He wants *to tell the tale … anew* (line 5) but *anew* can mean again rather than fresh and new.

9 **A**: Churchill says *I have tried … to show the point of view appropriate to my years, whether as a child, a schoolboy …* (lines 7–9).

B: See A above.

C: Churchill says that the opinions expressed may *conflict with those now generally accepted* (line 10).

D: The book does not contain many *modern pronouncements* (line 12).

10 **C**: Churchill speaks of *these anxious and dubious times* (line 23) and says they are *very different* (line 23) from what has gone before when *the dominant forces in Great Britain were very sure of themselves* (line 19).

A: This answer depends on a misreading of *violent domestic revolution* (line 16).

B: Churchill says *I was a child in the Victorian era, when the structure of our country seemed firmly set* (lines 17–18). This implies stability, but there is no indication of subsequent instability.

D: Churchill says *they were sure they were supreme at sea and consequently safe at home* (lines 21–22), but there is no indication of subsequent lack of safety. (Both halves of the proposition in the question need to be borne out by evidence. In C they are, but in B and D only one of them is.)

11 **A**: The question refers to the final sentence of the second paragraph which in turn refers back to the second sentence where the answer may be found. (The rest of the paragraph is mainly concerned with expanding this idea.)

B: Churchill speaks of *these anxious and dubious times* (line 23) but he is not referring to personal anxiety and doubt.

C: Churchill says that opinions in the book may *conflict with those now generally accepted* (line 10) but this is stated and disposed of in the first paragraph and does not tie in with the reference to readers (line 24) at the end of the second paragraph.

D: Again, this comes from the opening paragraph and does not tie in with the second.

12 A: The words *even, yet* and *nonetheless* (lines 31–32) convey Churchill's surprise and pinpoint what surprises him.

B: Churchill's first memories are *a child's first thoughts and ideas* but he doesn't claim that they throw special light on the way a child thinks.

C: Only some of Churchill's memories are *clear and vivid* (line 32) and he doesn't seem particularly struck by their quality. (The intensifying word *so* is in the question only, not in the passage.)

D: They may often be of ordinary people and things but he doesn't seem particularly struck by this. In fact he doesn't even point it out.

13 B: Churchill says *I have tried ... to show the point of view appropriate to my years, whether as a child, a schoolboy ...* (lines 7–9).

A: See B above.

C: There is no evidence for this.

D: Churchill says *I have most carefully verified my facts from the records which I possess* (lines 6–7), but he would not have had records to show the truth of a statement like this.

14 D: Churchill speaks of the family's *official residence* (lines 34–35).

A: See D above and consider, too, the driving to the castle (line 35) where family friends apparently live.

B: There is no evidence for this.

C: The reference to the *castle* (line 35) could suggest this, but the castle is evidently not in use as a military stronghold.

FURTHER PRACTICE AND GUIDANCE

Questions 8 and 9
The key to question 8 in the test is **a** (**b** comes later in the paragraph, where Churchill is describing his approach to the task and the care he took; however, his basic purpose appears at the outset, as we would expect, and **a** is central to this). The key to question 9 is **c**.

Question 10
They rested therefore sedately under the convictions of power and security. Very different is the aspect of these anxious and dubious times (lines 22–23) supports C. *They* (line 22) refers to *the dominant forces in Great Britain*, in other words the ruling class (line 19).

Question 11

1 Only A refers to the second paragraph.

2 The second paragraph is most likely to give the answer to the question.

Question 12
A

Question 13

1 The relevant statement is *I have tried ... to show the point of view appropriate to my years, whether as a child, a schoolboy ...* (lines 7–9).

2 The shortest sentences are in the passage about the pantomime visit (lines 33–40), and they go with a child's way of speaking or writing.

Question 14
A (least likely), B/C, D (most likely).

P94 PAPER 1 PART 3

15 E: The rest of the paragraph says why the book is perfect for the sort of people mentioned in E.

16 F: The reference to *this format* links with what has gone before, while the second half of the sentence relates to what follows.

17 G: This sentence says precisely what the writer wanted more of.

18 A: *The results* (line 23) mentioned at the start of the third paragraph are obviously the results of this research.

19 D: Only D, referring to *some of the chapters*, provides the right context for *such chapters* (line 31) in the sentence that follows.

20 C: The *either* suggests that the missing passage gives a second reason for omitting some words. It must therefore follow a sentence that gives a (first) reason, and this is the case with the sentence just before the gap.

21 B: *Speaking of digestibility* echoes *easier-to-digest* (line 43) in the previous sentence.

P95–96 PAPER 1 PART 4

For Part 4, see also **Further Practice and Guidance** on pages 97–98 and the answers below.

22 A: Mountain bikes are described as *the cheapest* (line 4).

23 B: *The power pack recharges overnight at a cost of only a penny or two* (lines 27–29). (Purely pedal-powered bikes are even cheaper to run, but the question must be answered *according to the information given*.)

24 A: *Mountain bikes are ... capable of bouncing down rocky paths without suffering any ill effects* (lines 6–9).

25 C: Comparison is made with mountain bikes, and the paragraph continues *the contact with the road or track is that much less and the route and manner of cycling need adjusting with regard to safety* (lines 40–43).

26 D: Tandems are said to be *wasteful of effort* (line 55). See also the last two sentences of paragraph D (lines 62–67).

27 B: The words *assisted* and *electric* should discourage E. The *'booster'* (line 17) simply helps (or assists) in propelling the rear wheel, while the fact that *the power pack recharges overnight* (lines 27–28) implies the use of electricity.

28, 29 A, D (in any order): *Mountain bikes are strong, resilient machines* and a tandem is a *heavy machine – just a little too 'chunky' for some people's liking* (lines 6–7, 52–53).

30, 31 A, B (in any order): A explains that thanks to the gears *getting to the top (of a hill) shouldn't prove too difficult* (lines 13–14) and B refers to gentle help with propulsion up hills (lines 23–25).

32, 33 B, E (in any order): Note the references to *light fingers* (line 32) and *envious eyes* (line 81) (both of which are figures of speech referring to those who are tempted to steal).

34, 35 C, E (in any order): Racing cycles offer *speed, so a greater distance can be covered in a day* (lines 44–46) and motor bikes offer *maximized* (line 71) speed and the potential for feeling the wind in the hair (line 75).

FURTHER PRACTICE AND GUIDANCE

Questions 22 and 23
The answers are in **a** (line 4) and **c** (lines 27–29).

Question 24
A and C are the two relevant paragraphs.

Question 25
C says this, and the reason is safety (or, more precisely, that racing bikes have poorer grip on the road surface).

Question 26
The paragraph says that tandems are efficient (ie energy saving) when ridden by two, but require great effort when ridden by one.

Question 27
Assisted means that the rider must still put some effort in – the motor or engine does not do all the work. The mention of a *power pack* (line 27) and recharging (line 28) indicates the use of electric power.

Questions 28 and 29
The adjectives are *strong, resilient* (line 7) (A) and *heavy* (line 52) and *chunky* (line 53) (D).

Questions 30 and 31
A has *a good range of gears* (lines 11–12) which means that *getting to the top ... shouldn't prove too difficult* (lines 13–14). B has a *'booster' device* (line 17) which the rider puts into action to help him *when uphill stretches present themselves* (lines 24–25).

Questions 32 and 33
The expressions are *those with light fingers* (line 32) (B) and *envious eyes* (line 81) (E).

Questions 34 and 35
C and E refer to *speed* (lines 45 and 71) and E refers to the sensation of the wind in the hair (line 75).

P101 PAPER 2

FURTHER PRACTICE AND GUIDANCE

Assessment of sample answer

1 Overall, the story fulfils the question, although the given sentence is near the end rather than at the end. The second paragraph does nothing to carry the story forwards and a better alternative would have been to expand the third paragraph. Perhaps Jimmy could have argued and insisted there was no danger just before having his accident.

2 The story is well organized, with nothing out of place, and the paragraphing is correct. There is an introductory paragraph designed to raise interest – *our holiday[s] were [not] as we had planned* – a paragraph of (needless) detail, a paragraph containing the key event and a paragraph consisting of memory and comment.

3 The first two sentences are correct in basic structure. The first is a simple 'opener' and the second is far more complex, which makes a pleasant contrast. However, the third paragraph begins with an ill-formed sentence and it includes a pair of clauses – *Jaime picked him up. we arrived at a village* – that are not linked to one another or to anything else. The style here is very immature.

4 The vocabulary is barely adequate, though the mention of *animals, reptil[es] and insects* is pleasing.

5 There are serious grammatical flaws, especially in the use of verbs and nouns, where singular forms are sometimes used for plurals. However, *the girls swam in the lake* and *our things weren't there* are examples of number and

tense used correctly. One can only make sense of the student's second sentence by assuming that he/she has accidentally omitted *not* (see 2 above).

6 The style is appropriate.

P102 PAPER 3 PART 1

For Part 1, see also **Further Practice and Guidance** on page 103.

1 **A**: *Born and brought up* is a common phrase. B and C could have been used in the absence of *up*. D could be used in a phrase like *if I'd grown up in Norfolk*, but not in the passive construction *someone (who was) born and … up in Norfolk*.

2 **D**: *On the contrary* is an idiomatic phrase like *on the other hand*. A suggests the correct meaning but is not an acceptable turn of phrase. B and C create meaningful phrases (*on the whole* and *on the evidence*) but they are inappropriate in the context.

3 **C**: D is also possible but *has to give* is more appropriate when speaking of a person rather than a county.

4 **A**: *Elsewhere* is the only word suggesting an alternative place.

5 **C**: Numbers are said to be *low* or *small* (or *high* or *large*).

6 **B**: *Because* suggests a direct link between fewer people and less pollution. The other options suggest that there is some sort of contrast between the two ideas.

7 **B**: *Running* is frequently used to refer to the course or route which something takes as in *there was water running down the wall*.

8 **B**: *Little* is the appropriate word to use in conjunction with an uncountable noun like *traffic*. A (*few*) would go with a countable noun like *vehicles*. C might be used with singular abstract nouns like *disturbance* as in *disturbance from traffic noise was slight*, while D (*scarce*) refers to something which is in short supply compared with demand as in *fruit was scarce* or *potatoes were scarce*.

9 **A**: *In addition* is the only phrase that has an appropriate meaning, though the other options give phrases which could be used in other contexts.

10 **D**: *Along* is better than C (*beside*) because it goes with the fact that the coast extends a very long way.

11 **A**: The other options could fit into the immediate context but not the broader context. It is important to consider whole sentences and even whole paragraphs.

12 **C**: B (*accompany*) is the appropriate choice if there is progression or movement. Thus a piano (or pianist) accompanies a singer during the progression from start to end of a song, or someone accompanies a friend on a journey. A could be used in a context like *long distance footpaths along almost the whole of this coast offer excellent walking* and D could be used with an adverb as in *long distance footpaths*

run along almost the whole of this coast.

13 C: *Through* has an appropriate sense of looking in one end and out the other. B (*into*) is inappropriate because it has the opposite effect. It implies attention to something of interest inside the binoculars.

14 C: *Fears for* is idiomatic. None of the other options can be followed by *for*, A (*worries*) and D (*wonders*) requiring *about*. B (*dreads*) would normally be followed by a clause beginning *that*.

15 C: *Weary* is the only idiomatic choice in this context.

FURTHER PRACTICE AND GUIDANCE

See Part 1 above.

P104 PAPER 3 PART 2

16 on: This word sometimes suggests *resting on* as in *the flowers were on the table*. However, it also has quite abstract uses as in *she's always on his side if there's an argument*, *on the other hand* and *on my behalf*.

17 which: This word is used when referring back to something after *in, by, on, under*, etc.

18 in: Like *on*, this word has abstract uses as in *in an attempt*, *in case (of something)* and *in time* (see 19 below).

19 in: See 18 above. (*On time* is also an English phrase, but it refers to being punctual in relation to a pre-arranged time as in *the train was on time*.)

20 away: *Away from* is the opposite of *towards*.

21 as: *While* is wrong because it suggests a period of time rather than a moment.

22 through: *In* is just possible but it doesn't suggest the travel which is clearly involved in the passage.

23 do: This is used for emphasis. It makes the contrast with *don't*, used a little earlier.

24 no: The words *a* and *the* would fit grammatically but do not respond to the sense of the passage.

25 asking: *Enquiring* is just possible but it sounds too formal and polite for the context. *Saying* is also possible and could suggest that the hearer is dazed by the accident and does not realize that he/she is being asked a question.

26 at: *At* is used with expressions of time to refer to two things coinciding as in *at the very moment I knocked at his door he was knocking at my door*.

27 head: *Head and shoulders* is a common phrase and clearly makes sense in the present context.

28 at: One is angry *with* a person but *at* an event or circumstance.

29 first: This depends on understanding the overall sense.

30 answered/replied: Words like *said* are rarely acceptable if one of these more specific words will fit.

P105 PAPER 3 PART 3

For Part 3, see also **Further Practice and Guidance** on page 106.

31 Until I've sold my house **I'm/I shall be unable to** move. (The choice between *I can't* and *I'm/I shall be unable to* applies whether the sentence is arranged the first way or the second way.)

32 I still **haven't received** my parcel. (*I haven't received my parcel yet* would also be grammatical.)

33 This is **the last warning I'll/I shall** give you.

34 All the plants in my garden **are dying because of/due to** the dry weather. (*Due to* is probably a little less natural here.)

35 He **was scared of/by** the mouse. (There is a slight difference of meaning between *scared of* and *scared by*. The latter suggests that the mouse did something to scare him.)

36 He couldn't **stop in time to avoid** the accident.

37 The carrots **appeared to be** bad.

38 I **asked the way because** I was lost.

39 I'm **so hungry I could eat** two lunches.

40 The return fare **is/costs twice (as much as)** the single fare.

FURTHER PRACTICE AND GUIDANCE

See Part 3 above.

P107 PAPER 3 PART 4

41 ✓

42 ✓

43 the: It would only be right in a context like *the larger the flowers, the better*.

44 be: Again, the context is all-important – *can best be done* would be correct.

45 ✓

46 you: This is tricky because *they'll last you for years* without the *sometimes* and *on end* would be acceptable. With the *sometimes* and *on end* the emphasis is on the flowers, not on the person, and the *you* is therefore inappropriate.

47 up: It implies getting rid of a surplus rather than using something carefully.

48 ✓

49 of: *Of which the sender has made the design by hand* would be correct but the second *of* in this line is not correct in the sentence as it stands.

50 such: See 51 below.

51 so: Note that omitting *such* and *so* makes the sentence much clearer and simpler.

52 off: *Better off* means having more money.

53 ✓

54 ✓

55 why: *Why* goes with asking or stating a reason and this is not being done in the passage.

P108 PAPER 3 PART 5

For Part 5, see also **Further Practice and Guidance** on page 109.

56 undoubtedly

57 fitness

58 vitality

59 moderation

60 greedily

61 Treatment

62 avoidance

63 choice

64 selection

65 reduction

FURTHER PRACTICE AND GUIDANCE

See Part 5 above.

P110–111 PAPER 4 PART 1

The line references are to the tape transcripts on pages 170–172.

1 **C**: He says *aren't you going to check me over?* (lines 17–18). A is wrong because it's the doctor who mentions wanting a prescription (lines 29–30) not Mr Jones (and *want* in this context has the colloquial meaning of *need* or *have forgotten*). B is wrong because Mr Jones just says *I might need hospitalization!* (lines 20–21).

2 **C**: The receptionist says *I'll put you down for a thorough inspection* (lines 17–18) (suggesting A) but she goes on to say that she'll *leave*

room in the appointment book (lines 18–19) so that Mr Brownlow can *stay in the chair* (lines 19–20) for all his treatment. B is wrong because although the receptionist suggests Mr Brownlow's treatment could fill *half a dozen spells in the chair* (lines 24–25), this isn't what she offers him.

3 **B**: The reference to *chasing rabbits* (line 15) and the suggested names *Gnasher* (line 16) and *Growler* (line 17) establish that it's a dog, not a cat or a child, and the final sentence confirms this.

4 **B**: It is most unlikely that you will know the word *terpsichorean* (line 5) but this does not matter. The balance of the evidence still points to dancing.

5 **B**: *Yes I know I can have my money back but* are the key words here. He doesn't refuse an apology (A), though he receives it ungraciously. As for a fresh delivery (C), this is what he accepts.

6 **B**: The man mentions a parked van (lines 14–15).

7 **A**: Clues include the mention of his *voice* (line 2) and *vocal art* (line 8).

8 **C**: When Alice says they could *go to the reception inside our shopping* (lines 13–14), she means they can wear the new clothes they might buy.

P111 PAPER 4 PART 2

The line references are to the tape transcripts on page 173.

9 Windsor (line 5)

10 travel(ling) by coach and train (lines 9–10)

11 motor bike (lines 13–14)

12 (all) the fumes and noise (on the road) (lines 14–15)

13 coach (line 16)

14 one and a half hours/an hour and a half (lines 20 and 26–28)

15 got on the wrong tube train/a tube train going in the wrong direction/went the wrong way on the underground (railway) (lines 23–25)

16 she didn't have time/would have missed another coach if she'd (tele)phoned (lines 35–37)

17 (tele)phones/better catering (facilities) (on board) (lines 38–41)

18 had a meal/eaten (lines 43–44)

P112 PAPER 4 PART 3

The line references are to the tape transcripts on page 174.

19 C: The passage mentions *attending to the engine* (line 5), and there are several indications of an unwanted delay. The words *guard* (line 3), *engine* (line 5) and *connections* (line 7) collectively point to a train.

20 D: Again, there are numerous indications of a breakdown.

The word *hydrofoil* (line 2), indicating that a boat is involved, may not be familiar, but other indications of the form of transport are the *up and down movement* (caused by the swell) (lines 5–6) and the mentions of the *tug* (line 8) and the *port* (line 9).

21 A: The mention of *the upper deck* (line 1) and of a driver giving a commentary (lines 6–7) indicates travel by bus or coach. Moreover, the journey is clearly by land and is contrasted with travel by train, which is thus ruled out.

22 B: The contrast with travel by car rules out E, and the mention of *leg power* (line 5) and *exhausting* uphill stretches (line 7) indicates B.

23 F: This answer is indicated by the words *parked* (line 1), *something wrong* with *the clutch* (lines 4–6), *the motoring organization* (line 7) and *the mechanic* (line 11).

P112 PAPER 4 PART 4

The line references are to the tape transcripts on pages 175.

24 C: She has to repeat to the manager what is wrong with the disc.

25 M: *Because head office hasn't provided … a CD player in the shop* (lines 30–31).

26 C: She says she *can definitely assure* the manager that she's right about what music is on the disc (lines 32–33).

27 A: She warns the manager and the customer that *there's ice all over the pavement outside* (line 40).

28 C: She cannot believe there is ice on the pavement in midsummer (lines 41–42).

29 A: The manager praises her courage (line 52).

30 M: He apologizes for taking a lot of the customer's time (lines 53–55).

FURTHER PRACTICE AND GUIDANCE

1 **1 C, 2 D, 3 E, 4 F, 5 G, 6 A, 7 F, 8 B**

2 **1 F, 2 H, 3 G, 4 B, 5 A, 6 D, 7 C, 8 E**

LISTENING SCRIPTS

TEST 1   PART 1

You will hear people talking in eight different situations. For questions 1–8, choose the best answer, A, B or C.

QUESTION 1

Customer: I'm having to bring this paint back, I'm afraid. As soon as I opened the tin I began to cough and sneeze. I seem to be allergic to it. It's not the fault of the paint – it's me. I'm
5   the same outdoors in the summer – running eyes, sore throat ... you know, the whole works. But I'm frightened that if it goes on the walls I'll be coughing and sneezing for as long as I live there. Perhaps you've got some other
10   sort. As a matter of fact I could do with a slightly darker pink.

QUESTION 2

Woman: No more trains till seven o'clock? But I thought the service was every hour ... It is every hour – or it was last week. I'm sure there was one at five past six.

5   **Man**: Last week, you say. Which day did you travel – Friday, Saturday, Sunday, Monday?

Woman: Well, I really don't know. It was last weekend ... There must be a train – there's always one at five past six.

10   **Man**: I'm sorry, madam, not on a Sunday.

Woman: Look, this really isn't good enough. It's always one thing or the other ... delays, cancellations, whatever next? I want to see the station manager.

QUESTION 3

Man: I'm sure the weather's getting warmer.

Woman: What, today you mean?

Man: No, over the years. We used to have snow in April, even in May some years. Now it hardly
5   snows at all, even in the depth of winter. I bet it's that greenhouse effect they keep talking about.

Woman: Oh, global warming! What absolute rubbish! Look outside at the frost on the grass – and this is June.   10

Man: You see, you don't expect frost in June. Your expectations have changed with the years.

QUESTION 4

Policeman: I'm sorry, madam, but I must ask you to refrain from driving this car until the exhaust has been repaired.

Woman: But that's ridiculous. I've only just had a new exhaust fitted. You can see it's new.   5

Policeman: But I'm referring to the actual emissions, not the pipe itself. It's all down to how the engine's tuned – efficient combustion of petroleum products, as they say.

Woman: But officer, I had the engine tuned only   10 last week. It cost me nearly forty pounds.

Policeman: The fact remains that under the Road Traffic Act it's an offence to emit – what do they call it? – noxious fumes.

Woman: Meaning?   15

Policeman: Meaning up to a hundred pound fine if you don't comply.

Woman: Oh, very well.

QUESTION 5

Gardener: Look at mine. If I rub the soil off, you can see what a lovely golden colour they are. I put them in at the end of March and here I am in mid-July with the biggest crop I've had in my life. The harvesting usually breaks my back   5 but this time I was so delighted to have such a lovely heavy crop that the heaviness actually kept me going. It's all in the mind! Get them in early, that's the secret. I'll enter them for the local show – if they keep till September.   10 That's if my family don't eat them first.

QUESTION 6

Lecturer: ... of course, it changed the way in which people lived. Instead of growing their own food locally they had to start going to shops and markets. Everything was centralized
5 and controlled by others. What is more, the general standard of health declined drastically. Diseases struck overcrowded areas where people did not have so much as a pocket handkerchief plot on which to grow their
10 potatoes and onions. And you have to remember that doctors in those days did not have the antibiotics and other medicines which they have today. Look at the Royal Infirmary only a mile or so from here where we are now ...

QUESTION 7

Music critic: ... and then there's a majestic passage leading to a stately coda, which also serves as an archway into the final movement. Look out for the brass and muted strings,
5 restrained at first but blossoming, flowering, even richer and more colourful as time goes on. I think it's the grandeur I most admire – the sense of space and architecture. Everything's so well proportioned, and themes
10 and motifs follow on from each other with a seamless continuity.

QUESTION 8

Woman: I'd like to make a reservation, please. For *It Takes Two to Tango*. I'd like the members' discount, please ...

Oh dear, you mean you're fully booked.

5 It can't have done. Whatever's gone wrong?

In hospital! Oh! Well, I hope it isn't anything serious.

The people who've already booked must be terribly disappointed.

10 Yes, I'm sure you'll give them their money back. But what about members of the Theatre Club – like me, for instance? I wouldn't have joined if I'd known this would happen. My discount isn't much use to me now.

TEST 1   PART 2

You will hear a conversation between a salesman and his customer. For questions 9–18, complete the notes which summarize what the speakers say. You will need to write a word or a short phrase in each box.

You now have 45 seconds in which to look at Part 2.

Salesman: Now, Mr Jones, I'd like to show you our new computer. It's the TX100, made in Japan.

Customer: Ah, yes. I was going to ask you about that. If it's made abroad, I might have trouble   5 in getting spare parts.

Salesman: Not at all, Mr Jones. Our head office in London keeps all the spare parts and also a number of loan machines so that in the most unlikely event of yours developing a serious   10 fault – and the even more unlikely event of our not being able to repair it on site – you'd have the use of a replacement for as long as you needed it.

Customer: Free of charge, you mean?   15

Salesman: Well, all our service is free for the first year. After that there's an annual charge you can pay for on-site service.

Customer: On-site service. In other words you'd continue to come to my office to carry out any   20 repairs?

Salesman: Yes, we would. It's all included.

Customer: How soon can you sort a problem out?

Salesman: We'll be with you in less than thirty-six   25 hours.

Customer: I've heard that sort of thing before. Excuse me if I sound a bit cynical, but I've had disappointments with other firms promising speedy service. They say they'll come within   30 twenty-four hours, forty-eight hours or whatever it is, but then when it comes to it they don't count weekends and holidays, and forty-eight hours can easily turn into ninety-six hours, or even longer.   35

Salesman: Don't worry, sir. When we say thirty-six hours we mean thirty-six hours. Ring us one morning and we'll be with you by the end of

the next afternoon. Holidays are no exception
40   except in so far as our customers themselves
sometimes don't want to have us call at those
times.

Customer: Well, it sounds very good. And the
annual fee?

45 **Salesman**: After the first year the fee is one
hundred and fifty pounds.

Customer: A hundred and fifty pounds a year. It
sounds an awful lot.

Salesman: Well, think of it this way. It works out
50   at less than three pounds a week, which
doesn't exactly break the bank. I'm sure you
agree with that, Mr Jones.

Customer: Well, up to a point. Ah! I also wanted
to ask about running costs, the price of paper
55   for the printer and that sort of thing.

Salesman: The paper costs about two pounds a
roll and there's about three hundred sheets
per roll.

Customer: Are your printers easy to use? You
60   see, we've managed without one up to now.

Salesman: They couldn't be easier. In fact,
they're entirely automatic.

Customer: Huh, why are there so many knobs
and buttons?

65 **Salesman**: Ah, I was just coming on to that.

TEST 1   PART 3

You will hear five different people talking about
the sort of books they like to read. For questions
19–23, choose from the list A–F what each one
likes to read. Use each letter only once. There is
one extra letter which you do not need to use.

You now have 30 seconds to look through Part 3.

Speaker 1: Well, I'm really not that keen on
reading of any sort. I suppose I like fiction
more than fact, but not just any old fiction. I'm
a history fan so I go for books that have been
around for quite some time. Costume drama   5
on telly, visits to stately homes at weekends
and the classic authors. I think that just about
sums me up! Some people call me a fuddy
duddy, though I do like to have a bit of spice
in my fiction.   10

Speaker 2: It's people I'm really interested in so
I'm always on the lookout for a good new
novel. Crime and thrillers appeal to me most,
especially if there's plenty of suspense and
mystery. Oh, and I've really enjoyed a novel by   5
a man called Robert Glück. It's called *Margery
Kempe* and it's just been published. It's based
on fact, though the author obviously changes
things for the sake of his story. And frankly I'm
a great believer in author's licence, as it's   10
called.

Speaker 3: I like a good mystery so I'm always
looking out for up-to-the-minute books with
the latest news about strange phenomena:
unidentified flying objects, weird or menacing
beasts roaming lonely mountainsides and   5
things like that. By the way, I do believe in the
yeti – the abominable snowman – you know,
though I just missed a sighting when I made
my visit to the Himalayas. I think I know all
there is to know about the unknown.   10

Speaker 4: Me, I'm very down to earth. You
know how I am with gadgets, engines, things
like that. In fact the only books I like are the
sort that help me to save on garage repair
bills. I'm always reading the latest do-it-   5
yourself guides for Sunday engineers – people
who spend their weekends underneath their
cars. All my books are covered in oil! And just
look at my hands, not to mention my clothes!

Speaker 5: There are people I admire very much. Brunel, for instance. Where did he get the technical skill to build – or design – those bridges, ships and railways etc? Or to take a
5 completely different person, Margery Kempe. She lived six hundred years ago and she tramped all over Europe to visit holy places, even when she was old and ill. I like to read real life stories of what people did and why
10 they were like they were. You know what I say – understand others and you'll understand yourself as well.

TEST 1   PART 4

You will hear a conversation between a man called Mr Jenkins, his son, Bill, and his neighbour, Mrs Smith. Answer questions 24–30 by writing J for Mr Jenkins, B for Bill or S for Mrs Smith in the boxes provided.

You now have 30 seconds to look through Part 4.

Mrs Smith: Hello, Mr Jenkins. I'm afraid I have a grumble to make. It's about your son – well, that football of his, to be precise.

Mr Jenkins: Don't say he's kicking it into your garden again, Mrs Smith.   5

Mrs Smith: Well, yes, I'm afraid it keeps coming over.

Mr Jenkins: I've told him not to play in the street. Look, here he comes now. I'll have this out with him once and for all. Bill, I want you here, 10 this minute.

Bill: What's wrong, Dad? Why are you looking so angry?

Mr Jenkins: Mrs Smith tells me you're still letting that football of yours go into her garden. 15

Bill: Oh, yes. Well, I'm sorry. Hello, Mrs Smith.

Mr Jenkins: It's no good standing there squirming, Bill. I thought we'd sorted all this out last year, you and your friends. Surely you've got the sense to know that you're 20 causing damage.

Bill: Well, yes, Dad. In fact this time we've caused more damage than usual ...

Mr Jenkins: Look what happened to Mrs Smith's daffodils when they were just coming out last 25 spring ... Ruined, absolutely knocked to pieces.

Mrs Smith: It isn't just the damage, it's their welfare too. It isn't safe to play in the street so I don't want you coming down too hard on him, Mr ...   30

Mr Jenkins: I told you then and I'll tell you again ...

Mrs Smith: Don't come down on him too hard, Mr Jenkins. I can't help feeling sorry for the lad. He paid for the damage with his pocket 35 money and then in the autumn he burst a new ball on the thorns of my roses.

Bill: Dad, this time we were kicking the ball up
and down the road to avoid it going into the
40   gardens. After it went on the daffodils we
stopped using Mrs Smith's gate as a goal. It
was just an unlucky bounce that took it over
the wall and onto the roses. Anyway, it didn't
do any harm that time, not to Mrs Smith's
45   garden. It was Mrs Smith's garden that
damaged my ball.

Mr Jenkins: You're being cheeky!

Bill: No, Dad, it's true. And now, today, it did an
even unluckier bounce ...

50   **Mr Jenkins**: Now listen to me, Bill. Once more
into Mrs Smith's garden and I'll stop your
pocket money for ... well, I don't know how
many months.

Mrs Smith: Bill, surely it's best if you play on the
55   recreation ground. It's not far to walk.

Bill: But there's just one problem, Mrs Smith.

Mr Jenkins: There can't be a problem. You don't
mean you youngsters haven't the strength to
walk half a mile.

60   **Bill**: Well, no, it's not that.

Mr Jenkins: Well, go to the recreation ground.

Bill: But Dad, Mrs Smith, my ball's in Mrs Smith's
front room.

Mrs Smith: What on earth do you mean, in my
65   front room?

Bill: It did another funny bounce. It's gone
through your window.

TEST 2   PART 1

You will hear people talking in eight different
situations. For questions 1–8, choose the best
answer A, B or C.

QUESTION 1

Mary: Hello, John.

John: Hello, Mary.

Mary: How's your latest book going?

John: Oh, you mean the one I'm writing on the
Loch Ness monster? Well, it's going rather   5
slowly at present.

Mary: Oh dear. Why's that?

John: Well, the inspiration's there but everything
else is wrong. One day I tire myself out with
the writing and the next day I can hardly keep   10
myself awake. On top of that my word
processor keeps breaking down.

Mary: Perhaps you need to take a week off.

John: Well, I'm going up to Scotland to do some
research for the book next week.   15

Mary: That should be nice, especially if you see
the monster! But you'll still have your mind on
your work the whole time.

John: That's true. In fact at this stage seeing the
monster would be a mixed blessing as I'd have   20
to rewrite and revise large chunks that I've
already done. But going away gives the
engineer a good chance to see where the
trouble is. By the time I get back my machine
should be free of all its gremlins, even if I'm   25
still under the weather.

QUESTION 2

Lecturer: Let's put it this way, some people can
and some people can't. It's all to do with
having an over-active brain or the opposite – I
won't say underactive but, well, quiescent.
Some of my patients say they just put their   5
heads on their pillows and they're off straight
away, while others spend hours counting
sheep, making tea – which isn't a very good
idea – or reading novels from cover to cover.
By the way, tea and coffee are bad because   10
they're stimulants. They keep the brain active,

and not just the brain but the body too. The caffeine they contain stimulates the stomach, the bladder and a number of other vital
15 organs. They're the last thing I'd recommend as a nightcap.

QUESTION 3

Witness: I last spoke to Mrs Enderby on Tuesday. Then the following day …

Barrister: Can you be more precise? Was it morning, afternoon, evening? Can you tell us
5 the hour?

Witness: Well, I find it hard to remember after all these weeks.

Barrister: But you've already told the court about some of the television programmes you were
10 watching – no memory problems there, it seems – which suggests that you spent the evening at home. In which case you must have seen the victim, Mrs Enderby, during the daylight hours and presumably noticed the
15 state of her hair.

Witness: I've already told you, I never noticed the state of her hair.

Barrister: The jury will form its own conclusions about the state of your memory, Mr Waterson.

20 **Witness**: There's nothing wrong with my memory.

Barrister: Unless, perhaps, it's a little selective. Now think again about that fateful Tuesday. Never mind what you want to remember,
25 what do you remember?

QUESTION 4

Woman: You can't be serious!

Man: Yes, I am. I've won the jackpot.

Woman: A million pounds. I still can't believe it.

Man: Well, how can I prove it? Wait till the
5 money comes tomorrow. I'll show you the cheque. In fact, I'll do more than that. I'll treat you. And I do mean treat you.

Woman: That sounds exciting.

Man: Oh yes, I'll have more than enough for
10 myself and I mean to look after all my friends.

Woman: Oh, I don't know what to say. I'm sorry I ever doubted your word.

Man: Oh, don't worry. You haven't offended me. As soon as I knew I was in the money I thought of you and I said to myself, 'I'll lash
15 out on Jean. I'll buy her a CD or a pair of slippers.'

Woman: Oh. Oh, well thanks. That's nice. That's very nice.

QUESTION 5

Lecturer: Now the booklist has all your necessary reading for the term. The exam will have six essay questions and I've divided the booklist up into six corresponding sections. If you read two or three books from each of the sections,
5 you ought to be quite well prepared – though you'll need to come to the classes too. I'd like to think that goes without saying.
Now buying a dozen books would cost you a hundred pounds, possibly more. I realize that
10 almost no one here could afford that sum so I've checked with the library and in certain cases ordered copies. These are the absolutely vital ones which you really do need to borrow or buy.
15 Divide yourselves up into twos and threes and some study one topic while others study another one. The library should then be able to supply the different groups in turn. But do make sure that you've covered the whole of
20 the syllabus by the end of the course. And don't forget the second-hand bookshop, which can often help you out if need be.

QUESTION 6

George: Oh no! That's the seventh golf ball I've lost this week.

Samantha: I don't think you're getting under them, George.

George: No, it's not that. It's this awful club.

5

Samantha: It looks fine to me.

George: I'll show you, Samantha. Look straight along it. No, not like that. I'll hold it for you. Yes, that's better. Now can't you see the way it's bent?
10

Samantha: ... Well, not really. In fact, to be honest, no, not at all.

George: Well, it could be the fact that I've lost a lens from my glasses. Hang on, let me try
15   holding out my arm. Oh dear, my arm looks bent as well.

Samantha: I think that could be the answer, George.

QUESTION 7

Mr Fergusson: There are various things to consider when you're moving house. There'll obviously be a limit to what you can afford, but how can you get the best value for
5   money? Lower-priced houses sometimes gain in value faster than higher-priced ones. Buy just before this happens and you're getting a bargain. The gap between cheaper and dearer narrows. Then, a few years later, it opens up
10   again as the dearer houses pull away and regain their true value. In which case it's the dearer ones that reward the timely purchaser.

Interviewer: That's all very well, Mr Fergusson, but in practice people are very restricted in
15   their choice. A buyer with several children and a job to go to in a certain part of the country at a certain point in his career is to all intents and purposes forced to buy a house of a certain size in a certain place and thus at a
20   roughly pre-set price. It comes down to force of circumstances, not free choice.

Mr Fergusson: But there can still be an element of wise investment. The wise purchaser can always consider the state of the market.
25   Sometimes it may be wiser to rent a house for a while ...

QUESTION 8

Reporter: The incident happened on a Thursday night just before midnight. The man was reported to have left the club in Mount Street and run down the High Street shouting. On
5   reaching the Market Street fountains he waded to the central island and jammed a flagpole into the water jet, thus putting the fountain out of action. He later said he was raising the flag of freedom as a protest over
10   rising water bills.
The police surrounded the fountain and

waited for the man to return to the edge. He received a caution but later claimed that the police were acting outside their powers since the fountain is private property.   15
Responding to claims that the fountain wasted precious water, a council spokesperson pointed out that the water is constantly cycled by a hidden pump. The spokesperson declined to comment on the cost of the electricity   20
needed to drive the pump.

TEST 2   PART 2

You will hear a man called Mike telling you about his plans for the evening. For questions 9–18, complete the notes which summarize what he says. You will need to write a word or a short phrase in each box.

You now have 45 seconds to look at Part 2.

Mike: Hello, I'm Mike. Jill has just phoned to say that she's coming to visit me. She should arrive just after four o'clock.

So here I am at the Tourist Information Office.
5   I wanted to call at lunchtime but they were closed and I've had to wait until two o'clock. They've given me some leaflets and I've bought myself a local paper. I want to find somewhere good for us to go tonight.
10   Jill used to be mad on music and dancing. And me, I was always keen on sport, well, watching it on television, anyway. Jill was the one who went in for all the exciting things like skiing down mountains.
15   There are plenty of restaurants, but the food isn't always all that good and I probably can't afford it anyway.

Oh dear, I don't know what to choose. Ah, this looks good. There's a guided tour of the
20   local television studios. If you're lucky you can actually see some of the stars filming new episodes of soap operas and things. What does it say here in the small print? 'Small groups only, who have to watch from behind
25   a glass screen.' That sounds OK to me as long as there aren't loads of other people, in which case they probably won't let anyone watch at all.

Oh yes, and there's the Science Museum. Jill
30   says she doesn't like science but I've been on about taking her there for years and she is quite keen on the hands-on exhibits. There's a room where all the walls are distorted and painted with misleading lines, and the
35   furniture is all the wrong shapes and sizes. It deceives your eyes and the funny thing is that you stumble about and bump into things. Jill says it wouldn't happen to her. She thinks she's got a superior sense of balance or
40   something. But she just doesn't know what it's like in there. I'd certainly love to prove her wrong.

Oh dear, the Science Museum closes at five each evening. That's not very good. Oh well, we can go tomorrow but that still leaves
45   tonight to plan. I wonder whether she'd like to go and see Herbert and Muriel. She likes music, so why not spend the evening with two really top-class professionals?

TEST 2   PART 3

You will hear five people talking about memorable experiences they have had. For questions 19–23, choose from the list A–F what happened to each one. Use each letter only once. There is one extra letter which you do not need to use.

You now have 30 seconds to look through Part 3.

Speaker 1: And then it happened. The rope – I think you call it the painter, don't you? – well, it suddenly came away and I was completely adrift. I remember looking towards the weir
5   and thinking, 'I'll go over there if I'm not careful.' Careful – that's a joke for a start! What could I possibly do? I was helpless. Well, I reached the edge – I was terrified, I can tell you! – but I didn't go over. I just stayed at
10   the brink, broadside on, in the middle of all the swirling foam. And that's when I heard the sound of the klaxons. They didn't send just one appliance, there were three altogether, which excited all the crowds of children and
15   added to my total and utter embarrassment. They waded out in their welly-type things and pulled me ashore. I did feel a fool!

Speaker 2: Of course, I can't complain. It went off just like a fire extinguisher should and it's my fault I hadn't read the instructions. So the foam was all over my face and clothes. And
5   then the firemen started with their foam, not knowing I was inside the shop. I'm told I looked like a clown at the end of a circus act. And because I was really the cause of it all, I was hauled before the manager and given my
10   marching orders, which was harsh but not completely unfair. So that's why I'm looking for another job. But anyway, I've learned my lesson. There sometimes can be smoke without fire.

Speaker 3: Well, I was just walking along the pavement minding my own business, when this fellow working overhead caught the tin with his foot. And just when I thought I'd
5   managed to dodge the thunderstorm I was drenched with the stuff! I wasn't just daubed, I wasn't just splattered, I was covered in it from head to foot. And it came right through my suit to my skin. So I was red three times
10   over: red with rage, red with embarrassment and red – a sort of fashion shade – with all this oozing, sticky mess.

Speaker 4: I've never known such a deluge! It was trickling down my neck and filling my pockets and boots. It was just as though I'd taken a fully clothed dip in the lake. And that's when I had my great idea. I found this big sack
5   lying just on the bank. It was full of holes and I pulled it over my head. It was just as good as some of the latest fashions from Paris. Isn't there such a thing as a sack dress? It was still coming down like a waterfall but I
10   found a launderette, went inside and managed to get my clothes off from underneath the sack. So I sat there like a load of potatoes and watched my clothes tumbling round and round inside the machine. I could
15   have done with a bit of tumble drying myself. But at least I was under cover at last.

Speaker 5: It went all over me – I'm not joking. It wasn't just a case of being caught red handed, I was fluorescent red from head to toe. I've never been so embarrassed in all my life. Do you know, they had to close the shop and
5   throw half the stock away; the red was over everywhere. Of course the brief case people will pay for the damage. All I was doing was carrying it, minding my own business and doing my shopping so there was no reason at
10   all for the security canister to go off like a fire extinguisher. In fact it was more like a bomb it was all so sudden and quick.

TEST 2   PART 4

You will hear a conversation which takes place on a busy pavement between an inspector from the government, a woman called Mrs Turnbull and a woman who is passing by. Answer questions 24–30 by writing I for inspector, T for Mrs Turnbull or P for passer-by in the boxes provided.

You now have 30 seconds to look at Part 4.

Passer-by: What are you people doing here with all these placards? You're blocking the pavement! I can't get past!

5 **Mrs Turnbull**: Didn't you read about it in the paper? An inspector's coming today to look at the traffic in the town and decide whether we should have a new relief road.

Passer-by: Well, that's splendid news. We really could do with that relief road. The traffic along
10 Main Street's absolutely horrendous. And the fumes, the pollution! They're killing the town. A quarter of the shops are closed already. I hope you manage to persuade the inspector. The sooner we get that road the better!

15 **Mrs Turnbull**: But we aren't demonstrating for the road. We're against it.

Passer-by: But that's absolutely ridiculous! You can't possibly want to rob the town of its new road! That's absolutely stupid!

20 **Mrs Turnbull**: The inspector's here. And the MP. And the TV cameras. Good. Now we'll tell him!

Passer-by: Yes, and I'll give him a piece of my mind, too. Excuse me, Inspector!

25 **Inspector**: Ah, you must be Mrs Turnbull. You're meeting me here to speak against the relief road, aren't you?

Passer-by: Certainly not! I'm an ordinary citizen and I'm very much in favour of the road, I can
30 assure you. Let me tell you …

Inspector: I'm sorry, Mrs Turnbull, but I came here to meet the official representatives of those bodies with a particular interest in this project. I haven't time to speak with every
35 passer-by.

Passer-by: But I have a particular interest. And my name's not Turnbull. It's …

Mrs Turnbull: No, but mine is. I'm Mrs Turnbull, Inspector, and I'm here to speak on behalf of the Bradley Action for Tunnel Transport group. 40

Inspector: Ah, I've had some correspondence from you, haven't I? Your group wants the road to be driven through a tunnel instead of along the proposed route between the railway and the canal. But, you know, the cost of your 45 scheme really would be prohibitive.

Mrs Turnbull: But this is a narrow valley and the proposed relief road would create more traffic, not less. You'd only be moving the existing main road by a few hundred yards. People in 50 the town already suffer from asthma and other lung disorders. Has the government considered the long-term cost of caring for all these ill people?

Inspector: The government considers the cost in 55 accordance with established guidelines.

Mrs Turnbull: But do those guidelines include directives from the EU? What about the environmental considerations, for example? There are several rare species of wild flower 60 that will be totally destroyed if this road goes ahead.

Inspector: The road could be raised over any sites of special interest.

Mrs Turnbull: On stilts, you mean? But think of 65 the damage putting those in will cause. No, a tunnel's much the best solution.

Passer-by: So you'd put off this road, which is vital for our town, just for the sake of a few miserable flowers? People are far more 70 important!

Inspector: Mrs Turnbull, please! I can't talk to you. I have to listen to what this representative of BATT has to say. I must be fair.

Passer-by: Well, it's not fair if you won't listen to 75 the ordinary voter in the street. I shall write to the papers about this! At least they've got the intelligence to get my name right.

TEST 3   PART 1

You will hear people talking in eight different situations. For questions 1–8, choose the best answer A, B or C.

QUESTION 1

Customer: It's the lining. Look here, you can see for yourself how it's coming unstitched. And I've only worn it once or twice. It's as bad as the coat I returned last week. I don't really
5   want another one in case it's the same. I live fifteen minutes' drive away – that's when I've got my car on the road. Today, with it being in the garage, I've had to come by bus. You can't expect me to spend my time bringing five
10   pound skirts back all the while. I'd best have a refund and try somewhere else.

QUESTION 2

Man: Ten o'clock? That's far too late. I need to catch the train at ten, so I need picking up at twenty to at the very latest. If you haven't got a driver available for me I'll just have to try
5   another firm. And if no one can help me, I may as well cancel the journey completely.

You'll arrange with another firm yourself? Well, that's extremely kind of you but why should you go to all that trouble?

10   Well, you certainly take good care of your regular customers. Goodbye for now, then, and thanks very much!

QUESTION 3

Dentist: I'm afraid you'll need two extractions, sir. These upper left molars …

Patient: But can't they be filled like they have been before?

5   **Dentist**: Yes, Mr Bates, you must be tired of coming for all those endless fillings. This time they're just too badly decayed to preserve any longer. Frankly, over the last few years they've been filled so much that there's not much left,
10   apart from the roots.

Patient: Good heavens! I'm not too keen on extractions.

Dentist: I'm fully booked for the next six weeks but if you want the work done sooner – if you find you're in any pain, for example – you may   15 be able to get an appointment with one of my colleagues.

QUESTION 4

Mother: Well done, Peter. This is far and away the best report you've had for years. Dad'll be pleased with the geography mark after all the help he's given you lately. Maybe it's finally paying off. Hmm … yes, they all say how hard   5 you're working … Even the maths! What's got into you, Peter?! Are you sure you've got the right report?! But I think the thing that'll please Dad most is the way you've gone ahead with your French. Here, you'd better have   10 some more cake – or should I say *gâteau*?

QUESTION 5

Instructor: Rum titi tum. Rum titi tum. You need to hold the drumsticks a little less firmly than that … That's it! So they pivot freely between your fingers.

Pupil: But I don't really like these exercises. I want   5 to go in for jazz, not this.

Instructor: But what does it matter? You need to sharpen up your techniques or you won't be able to drum at all. Now come on, John, don't hold those sticks like a hammer and chisel.   10 Hold them lightly and let them bounce off the skin of the drum. Concentrate on building up the pace and the rhythm.

Pupil: If I do it fast enough, it'll be like a drum roll.   15

Instructor: Exactly. That's what we're aiming at.

Pupil: I want to play the cymbals too.

Instructor: We'll come to that. We need to do one thing at a time.

QUESTION 6

Man: The main thing wrong with the job is the money.

Woman: I'd have said the pay was excellent.

Man: No, I mean taking it over the counter, cashing up at night, and so on.   5

Woman: That's not beyond you.

Man: It's the responsibility. If anything goes wrong they knock it off my wages. Suppose I accept a forged note. Even the schoolkids are up to it these days. One mistake and it's twenty – or even fifty – pounds gone from my own pocket.

Woman: Oh, don't be unfair. They're not all into crime. Far from it, in fact.

QUESTION 7

Travel agent: You can book an earlier flight from Amsterdam if you like. But there's not much point. You see, there'd be no connection when you got to Dresden. You'd just have to wait around for five hours. You may as well have a full night's sleep and complete the journey, well, between breakfast and your evening meal when you get to Moscow. OK? So you need to reach Amsterdam Airport for half past nine, which is more or less after the morning rush ...

QUESTION 8

Lecturer: Good evening, and I hope the people at the back can hear clearly. Can you? Good. Well, today I want to talk about the way the colours around us affect our moods and behaviour. Take blue, for instance. Blue's a fine colour for many things – a symbol of tradition, quality, stability. As such, it features on the Union Jack and the flags of nations around the world. It's also the colour of the inimitable willow design on china from, well, from China, of course. But just imagine if all the food on your plate was blue – the colour nature has chosen for various fungi, moulds and deadly poisons.

TEST 3   PART 2

You will hear part of a talk about antique collecting. For questions 9–18, complete the notes which summarize what the speaker says. You will need to write a word or a short phrase in each box.

You now have 45 seconds in which to look at Part 2.

Antiques dealer: I'd advise anyone who's starting in antiques to begin very cautiously. It's very easy to spend a fortune on one or two items. They may be bargains or they may be rubbish, and the beginner obviously runs more risk than the seasoned collector of spending badly. But either way it kills the hobby instantly if all your money is locked up in just a couple of items.

No, you should go to local events – car boot sales, flea markets, even jumble sales – and spend a reckless pound or two on things that really take your fancy. And I do mean just a pound or two. I used to go to these events with a fiver, at most, tucked into my pocket. It stopped me giving way to any extravagant impulse and it also streamlined the bargaining process. When I said I only had a fiver on me the stallholders knew I was telling the truth – they're skilful judges of character – and either they accepted my meagre offer or they turned it down flat. We didn't waste each other's time. At these prices you don't need to be too selective, of course. Get them home, discuss them with friends, put them on show and find out all you can about them.

The beauty of this is that things that disappoint you you can quickly resell. Just go along to the sort of event where you got them in the first place. Offer them to stallholders or have a little stall of your own.

Things you obtained for a pound or two you can sell again for the same amount – perhaps a bit more – and then you can squander the proceeds in a further burst of reckless spending! Over the years you'll accumulate some startling bargains, but do it by sifting your way through the rubbish that comes along.

I think that's the answer. Don't go for quality, go for quantity. The more stuff you have passing through your hands the greater your

chance of a lucky find, yet you won't be taking any risks. Of course, you'll be gaining valuable
45 experience, skill and confidence. In the end you'll be able to spend big money, if you so desire, without making any major blunders. Do this to get treasured objects for your retirement home – crystal vases, grandfather
50 clocks and things like that.

That reminds me, don't forget to take out a suitable insurance policy – one that covers unspecified items for a high total value, as much as ten thousand pounds, perhaps. Like
55 that you can have things coming and going without the bother of insuring them specifically.

I can't think of anything else to say, just happy hunting!

TEST 3   PART 3

You will hear five different people talking about their hobbies. For questions 19–23, choose from the list A–F what each one does. Use each letter only once. There is one extra letter which you do not need to use.

You now have 30 seconds to look through Part 3.

Speaker 1: There are two ways to do it. One is to have no bottom on it and get the ship in that way. After which, of course, the bottom goes on with a little glue. But as far as I'm concerned that method is just for cheats – and 5 there's no use in having a hobby if it doesn't present a challenge! So now I'll tell you the proper way. Have the mast and rigging folded down on the deck of your ship like so. Can you see the one that I'm holding up? Good! 10 Then slip it in through the neck and gently pull on the cords. So up come your mast and rigging and you're almost home and dry.

Speaker 2: Then the things kept dying on me. They'd go brown round the edges which I thought was just due to lack of water. But that was only the start of the trouble. The rot would set in and before I knew it they'd be 5 totally useless. Of course, with all the different advice I got I was all at sea. Some said one thing and some said another. Old Charlie down the road recommended regular mulching all through the season, so that's 10 what I did. He said it had never been known to fail so I thought they'd recover – but no such luck. Look at these ones here.

Speaker 3: Take a look at my map – like most of my gear, I have it covered in plastic to keep the rain off, of course – and look at the plots of land strung out all along the valley. What the map doesn't show is the difference in 5 crops. First, at the lower levels, you find orchards and market gardens. Then, moving up, you come to the corn crops – the barley, the oats and that sort of thing. And finally, in the upper reaches, you come to the hill farms 10 with little other than pasture and sheep. It's the variety I like so much. Of course, toiling uphill can be a pain – literally at times. But striding (or should I say hobbling) back down at the end of the day makes it all worthwhile. 15

Speaker 4: For my business I chose a spot in the valley because that's where the soil is better, and there are fewer frosts and fewer high winds to blow the blossoms and ripening fruit
5 off the trees. But at weekends I really take to the surrounding hills in a big way. I've a good set of gears and with all the exercise I do in the gym I seem to have the pedal power to manage most gradients. I love to get off, sit
10 down for a rest and look from above at my patch of trees, especially when they're covered in blossom. Two wheels are definitely better than four when it comes to relaxing.

Speaker 5: People think it's an odd hobby because you can finish up in such a bad way – too tired to be good for anything else. I've a pedometer which I clip to my belt before I set
5 out. I've measured my average stride length – not when I'm flat out but at a fast trot – and I've keyed it in. So every time I try a new route it clocks up the miles and from that I can work out my average speed, assuming I look at my
10 watch when I start. I've been trying to build it up over the years but I think my age is against me now. Anyway, it's a healthy hobby – provided you don't overdo it, of course.

TEST 3   PART 4

You will hear a conversation which takes place at a second-hand shop between a taxi driver, his passenger Jenny and the woman called Ann who runs the shop. Answer questions 24–30 by writing T for taxi driver, J for Jenny or A for Ann in the boxes provided.

You now have 30 seconds to look through Part 4.

Taxi driver: You didn't have to get out of the car. I'd have been happy to collect it for you.

Jenny: Oh, thanks. But I haven't paid for it yet. Oh look, there's my chair – the one with my name Jenny on the label. Now, where's Ann? 5 Ah, in the back room. Excuse me, Ann!

Ann: Yes? Oh, yes, you've come for your chair, right?

Jenny: That's it. I've as good as bought it but the one thing we didn't do was agree on a price. 10

Ann: Make me an offer.

Jenny: A fiver?

Ann: Well, I don't think ... can't you do any better?

Jenny: Seven fifty, then. Cash. 15

Ann: Oh, go on, then.

Jenny: Here you are ... Six pounds, seven pounds, seven pounds fifty.

Ann: Thanks.

Taxi driver: Right, if the deal's complete I'll carry 20 it out to the car ... My goodness it's heavy!

Ann: Well, you'd better not grumble after the way I've recommended you to this lady like I do to all my customers. I told her Quickfire Taxis are very good at squeezing things into 25 their cars. Mind you, she says she knows you already and uses you all the time!

Jenny: Let me hold the door for you, Kenneth. Yes, you seem to have friends all over town. You know when you picked me up with my 30 shopping I was talking to Philip. Well, he says he recommends you too.

Taxi driver: Well, I helped him once or twice when he had a problem ... The thing is, if you want people to be friendly to you, you have to 35

be prepared to do things for them. Put
yourself out a little – carry their shopping, give
them a cheerful smile. Do you know, I have a
customer, an old lady, who pays me to drive
40   her into the country for an afternoon out. We
have tea at a café – she pays – and we come
home. She wants the company, that's all.

Ann: A good way to earn a living.

Taxi driver: Yes, very. I said to her, 'Look, you
45   shouldn't be spending all that money,' and she
got really fierce with me. 'It's my money,' she
said, 'and if I don't spend a bit in my old age
what'll happen to it? It'll only go to my heirs!'

Ann: Doesn't she care about her family, then?

50   **Taxi driver**: She hasn't any children. She's lonely.
That's why she likes to drive out with me.
Mind you, she doesn't always remember
where she's been!

Jenny: Well, I know where I'm going next. I need
55   a few home comforts after all this shopping.
It's time to put my feet up and have a jolly
good rest. You're sure you can get the chair
into the car?

Taxi driver: No problem. You sit in the front and
60   I'll shove it on the back seat.

TEST 4   PART 1

You will hear people talking in eight different
situations. For questions 1–8, choose the best
answer A, B or C.

QUESTION 1

Doctor: Now then, Mr Jones, what seems to be
the matter with you?

Mr Jones: Well, I've been suffering from
extremely bad stomach pains. I've hardly dared
leave the house!   5

Doctor: Hmm. Are you experiencing any
sickness?

Mr Jones: Of course I'm experiencing sickness!
That's why I'm here!

Doctor: No, no, Mr Jones, you misunderstand me   10
... Well, anyway, it's probably just a bug
you've picked up – nothing to worry about. I'll
give you some drugs to ease the symptoms,
and I suggest you go home and get plenty of
bed rest. If you don't show any improvement   15
in a day or two come and see me again.

Mr Jones: What? Aren't you going to check me
over?

Doctor: That won't be necessary.

Mr Jones: But what if I'm seriously ill? I might   20
need hospitalization! I might be dying!

Doctor: Now, now, Mr Jones. Let's not be
melodramatic. I'm sure there's nothing
seriously wrong with you.

Mr Jones: I could sue you for medical negligence.   25
I demand a second opinion! You can be sure I
won't be coming to this surgery again! Good-
day.

Doctor: Mr Jones! Come back! You want your
prescription!   30

QUESTION 2

Receptionist: What's that, Mr Brownlow? Can
you speak a bit more clearly, I can hardly make
out what you're saying ...

You want to make an appointment to see Mr
Pullem.   5

Your teeth are in a bad way, you say? How
long is it since your last inspection?

What's that? Three years! Well, Mr Brownlow,
I must say I'm not surprised your teeth need
10 attention if you haven't had them checked for
three years! Mr Brownlow, I can't tell you
enough how important it is for us all to have
our teeth checked regularly! If problems aren't
spotted early on, it can lead to decay, which
15 means fillings and even extractions, you know!
I expect you'll be needing a lot of fillings! I tell
you what, I'll put you down for a thorough
inspection but I'll leave room in the
appointment book so that you can stay in the
20 chair and Mr Pullem can do any fillings and
other work like extractions that might be
necessary. How does that sound, bearing in
mind that after this length of time you've as
good as stored up half a dozen spells in the
25 chair ...?

What's that Mr Brownlow?

Oh, I see. You've decided you don't want an
appointment at all ... He's rung off ... I wonder
what I said to upset him.

QUESTION 3

Old lady: Will my little Charlie be all right,
doctor?

Vet: Well, I've examined him thoroughly and I'm
pleased to say that Charlie is going to make a
5 full recovery. I've given him an injection and
cleaned the injury up a bit. Just make sure he
keeps off that bad leg until it's well. And keep
him out of fights from now on!

Old lady: Oh, dear. I do hope he'll be able to
10 manage all right! It will be terrible watching
him hobbling around the house. I do worry
about him so. He's such a naughty little boy!

Vet: You really shouldn't worry yourself. He'll
only be out of action for a short while. I'm
15 sure he'll be up and chasing rabbits again in
no time! Won't you, Gnasher! Sorry, what's
his name? Growler?

Old lady: No, no, no – this one's Charlie. Well,
thank you so much for taking such good care
20 of him. I'd better be off now. I want to buy
some steak for Charlie's tea before the
butcher shuts.

Vet: You're welcome. So that's what you've been
feeding him on, is it – steak! I wondered what
25 was making his coat so thick and glossy!

Old lady: Yes. Oh look, he's getting up! He must
be feeling better already! Oh you little darling!
Come along with Mummy, then. And this time
don't bark when you get on the bus, you
naughty boy!   30

QUESTION 4

Variety show host: For our next quite magical
performance, I would like to introduce a group
of incredible young men who are causing a stir
throughout England with their amazing – if
somewhat unusual – terpsichorean talents.   5
Ladies and gentlemen, I ask you to put your
hands (or if you prefer, your feet) together, for
the toe-tapping, madly-moving, proudly-
pirouetting, jazzily-jumping, fancy footwork of
The Bouncing Beans.   10

QUESTION 5

Market trader: Hello, is that Ferdinand's Fresh
Farm Foods? It's about the delivery I received
this morning. I have a complaint ...

What do you mean, what's the matter with it?
It's rotten, that's what the matter is! Call   5
yourselves Ferdinand's Fresh Farm Foods
indeed ...

I'm sorry, fine words and apologies are all very
well but I need some stock to sell at the
market!   10

What?

Yes, I know I can have my money back but
that won't keep my customers happy. I've got
a stall. It opens at ten and I've nothing to sell.
No, I tell a lie. I've got a ton of mouldy   15
potatoes, a ton of slimy carrots and two tons
of squashed tomatoes to sell, thanks to
Ferdinand's Foods! Not to mention the eggs
and the fruit ...

What?   20

Straight away?

Without further charge?

Oh! Well, thank you. Thanks very much
indeed.

QUESTION 6

Man: Gosh, there's a lot of damage here.

Woman: Yes. The man in the green car came out of that side street without indicating and ran straight into that red car that was just turning
5   in. It was all his fault.

Man: Oh, I'm not so sure. I think the red car was going too fast. Otherwise it would have stopped in time.

Woman: Anyway, how did the school bus and
10   the lorry get mixed up in this?

Man: The bus was coming up behind the red car and it had to brake suddenly to avoid it. So it spun out into the path of the lorry. I didn't see the actual smash because of that van that's
15   parked there in the way. I don't think anyone is hurt though, thank goodness.

Woman: Here come the police. Look, the children are fine. They're enjoying the adventure.

20 **Man**: Of course they are! Thanks to this they'll be having a day off school!

QUESTION 7

Chat show host: My next guest possesses a voice which has been described as 'an innovation' and also 'superbly original' by classical buffs and pop enthusiasts alike. His
5   unconventional rendering of the theme from Tchaikovsky's Violin Concerto, whilst technically brilliant, also brought a new meaning to the concept of vocal art. He has made a speciality of turning the old to the new
10 and making it accessible to all, this fact being reflected by the great success of his Catgut Rag, which is currently at number one in both the British and American charts. Ladies and gentlemen, it is my great pleasure to introduce
15 to you – Mr Nigel Cooke!

QUESTION 8

Alice: The wedding's at two and the reception's at seven. So there'll be a long gap between the two.

Peter: Yes, we could be stuck in a strange town
5   for ... four hours.

Alice: Well, I wouldn't say 'stuck'. It's a lovely town. We could do some shopping.

Peter: We can't turn up at the reception carrying bags, though, Alice. And we don't want to go trailing round the shops in our best clothes.   10

Alice: You're being awkward. We can put our shopping in our car. As for our clothes, we could even buy new ones, if it came to that, and go to the reception inside our shopping.

Peter: Well, I'm not too keen. It could be a very   15 expensive way of filling in time.

TEST 4   PART 2

You will hear a woman called Jean telling you about her journeys to Birmingham. For questions 9–18, complete the notes which summarize what she says. You will need to write a word or a short phrase in each box.

You now have 45 seconds in which to look at Part 2.

Jean: Hello, I'm Jean. I'd like you to meet my friend George. Come to that, I'd like to meet him myself. The trouble is that he lives in Birmingham, nearly a hundred miles from
5   here. He used to live in Windsor, just down the road from me, but he got a place to do theatre studies at Birmingham University and off he went on his motor bike!
So here I am at the travel agent's. I'm visiting
10 George – but should I go by coach or train? I've studied these leaflets but I'm finding it very hard indeed to make up my mind. One thing's for sure, I won't be going by motor bike! I don't know how George can bear all
15 the fumes and noise on the road!
Last time I visited George I found the coach very comfortable. It wasn't very convenient, though, making my way to Victoria Coach Station before I could really start my journey.
20 It took me an hour and a half to get to Victoria. First I had to get the train from Windsor to London, then I had to take the tube to Victoria. And guess what, I chose the wrong platform and went the wrong way,
25 heading back out in the Windsor direction. As a matter of fact it took me as long to reach Victoria as it did to get from Victoria to Birmingham.
George was waiting at Birmingham for the
30 coach to arrive. I'd expected to be an hour earlier but I'd missed that coach. He was really fed up by the time I finally made it. Part of the trouble was that I wasn't able to let him know about my mistake on the underground
35 railway. I could have phoned from Victoria but that would have meant missing another coach and being two hours late instead of one.
I wish they'd install phones on coaches. That's one way in which the train is better – you can
40 keep in touch. There's not much catering on coaches either. When I got to Birmingham I was famished. George had to take me straight home and feed me. Whichever way I travel this time I'll take care of that before I set off. I know it costs a lot in London, but it costs all   45
the more once you're on the move.

TEST 4   PART 3

You will hear five different people talking about their experiences on holiday. For questions 19–23, choose from the list A–F what happened to each one. Use each letter only once. There is one extra letter which you do not need to use.

You now have 30 seconds to look through Part 3.

Speaker 1: And then it stopped. We seemed to be standing there for ages. Then at last the guard came through – not in person, I mean he came through on the intercom. He said
5   they were attending to the engine. Something silly like a fuse I think he said it was. Of course, we were all concerned about our connections but what could we do? Just sit there and fume. It was one of those times when it
10   definitely *isn't* quicker by rail.

Speaker 2: The first I knew there was something wrong was when the hydrofoil cut out. Of course we came to a standstill almost at once. But when I say standstill I simply mean that we
5   stopped going forwards. The up and down movement became much more pronounced and I really disliked it – so did my stomach. Anyway, a tug came out and fetched us and took us into port – and not before time. I
10   don't think I'll travel like that again.

Speaker 3: It was smashing. From the upper deck I had a wonderful view of the scenery. By train you seem to spend half your time in tunnels and cuttings. Well, this was different. I could
5   see over all the hedges, and every twist and turn of the road gave a different view. The driver gave us a commentary on the main geological features and I feel I've learned a very great deal in the course of my tour.

Speaker 4: I really liked the wind in my hair. It was one of the biggest treats of my childhood – whizzing along in my uncle's sports car. Well, this was as good, except, of course, that
5   I had to supply the necessary leg power. The speed was less and the uphill stretches were very exhausting, but somehow I found it even more exhilarating than the motorized excursions I used to have with my Uncle Bill.

Speaker 5: So I've parked at the top of the cliffs and I'm enjoying the view. Who cares about a slight delay when the weather and the view are so stupendous? I knew there was something wrong because of the squeaking   5
noise whenever I let in the clutch. I rang the motoring organization and told them I'd try to get to Winterton Ness, which I've managed to do. Now it's a case of relaxing and letting someone else come and sort it out. I suppose   10
I'll have to stir myself when the mechanic turns up but till then I haven't a care in the world!

TEST 4   PART 4

You will hear a conversation in a shop between a customer, an assistant and the manager. Answer questions 24–30 by writing C for customer, A for assistant or M for manager in the boxes provided.

You now have 30 seconds to look through Part 4.

Customer: I'm afraid I have a complaint to make.

Assistant: Oh dear! What's the trouble?

Customer: It's this compact disc you sold me.

Assistant: Doesn't it work?

5 **Customer**: Oh yes, it works, but it's the wrong music.

Assistant: You've bought the wrong one?

Customer: Well, yes and no. The label says Rachmaninov and the disc itself says
10 Rachmaninov. But when I play it the music's Tchaikovsky.

Assistant: Are you sure?

Customer: Oh, yes! I can't be wrong about that. So I went through the motions of buying the
15 right disc and I've finished up with music I can't stand. Tchaikovsky's 1812 Overture – what a racket!

Assistant: I'll just go and fetch the manager for you.

20 **Manager**: Hello, madam. Can I help you at all?

Customer: Oh! Hasn't the assistant explained the problem?

Manager: No, and she's just going off for her lunch break.

25 **Customer**: I thought she was a bit eager to get away. It's this disc I bought here on Saturday. It says Rachmaninov but it's actually got Tchaikovsky on it.

Manager: Hmm, I wonder how we can check it.
30 I'm a bit irritated because head office hasn't provided us with a CD player in the shop.

Customer: Well, I can definitely assure you that I'm right. I know all the music. And there's no way there's any piano on this.

Manager: Well, the trouble is that I can't test any   35 replacement we give you. You might go away with the same thing again. Ah, hello Mary! That was a quick lunch break!

Assistant: I thought I'd just better tell you that there's ice all over the pavement outside.   40

Customer: That's impossible! It's the middle of summer!

Assistant: I think it's from the butcher's shop next door. He's defrosting his freezer or something.   45

Manager: Well, that's most annoying! It isn't the first time it's happened either! I'd better go and speak to him as soon as I've dealt with this customer.

Assistant: Would you like me to go? I know he's   50 a bit surly but he doesn't scare me.

Manager: That's courageous of you. Oh well, you can call in on your way to lunch. I'm sorry, madam, we seem to be taking a lot of your time. Well, the best thing we can do is to give   55 you your money back. Then you won't risk getting the same thing again.